W9-AGZ-226

DOUBLE YOUR
BRAIN POWER

INCREASE YOUR MEMORY BY USING ALL OF YOUR BRAIN ALL THE TIME

JEAN MARIE STINE

PRENTICE HALL
Paramus, New Jersey 07652

Library of Congress Cataloging-in-Publication Data

Stine, Jean.
    Double your brain power : increase your memory by using all of
your brain all the time / Jean Marie Stine.
    Includes index.
    ISBN 0–13–186719–9. — ISBN 0–13–186701–6 (pbk.)
    1. Intellect.   2. Brain.   3. Memory.   4. Thought and thinking.
5. Intellect—Problems, exercises, etc.   I. Title.
BF431.S742   1997
153—dc21   97–1633
                                                                        CIP

© *1997 by Prentice Hall, Inc.*

*All rights reserved. No part of this book may be reproduced in any form or by
any means, without permission in writing from the publisher.*

Printed in the United States of America

10 9 8 7 6 5 4 3 2

ISBN 0-13-186719-9   ISBN 0-13-186701-6 (pbk)

ATTENTION: CORPORATIONS AND SCHOOLS

Prentice Hall books are available at quantity discounts with bulk purchase for educational, business, or sales promotional use. For information, please write to: Prentice Hall
Career & Personal Development Special Sales, 240 Frisch Court, NJ 07652. Please supply: title of book, ISBN, quantity, how the book will be used, date needed.

PRENTICE HALL
Career & Personal Development
Paramus, NJ 07652
A Simon & Schuster Company

On the World Wide Web at http://www.phdirect.com

Prentice Hall International (UK) Limited, *London*
Prentice Hall of Australia Pty. Limited, *Sydney*
Prentice Hall Canada, Inc., *Toronto*
Prentice Hall Hispanoamericana, S.A., *Mexico*
Prentice Hall of India Private Limited, *New Delhi*
Prentice Hall of Japan, Inc., *Tokyo*
Simon & Schuster Asia Pte. Ltd., *Singapore*
Editora Prentice Hall do Brasil, Ltda., *Rio de Janeiro*

BF
431
.S742
1997

To

The Ladies of TCNE
Especially Brenda Burke, Nancy Cain, Jonel Peterson,
Gina Kamentsky and Alicia Carla Longstreet

and to

The Man of the House
Frankie Hill

ACKNOWLEDGMENTS

The author, [due to no doing of her own] was forced to move four times in the course of writing this book. As a result, she is unduly indebted to a number of people for assistance and patience throughout. First and foremost, Chris and Gurucharn, for buying and dropping off that bag of groceries. Richard F. X. O'Connor, for what he slipped into my pocket at the end of that visit. Merissa Sheryll Lynn, hostess and den mother *extraordinaire*. Yvonne Cook-Riley and the other good folk at the International Foundation for Gender Education, who granted me a much-needed vacation so I could finish this book. Brenda Burke for tender forbearance. The three editors at Prentice Hall who wore out in succession waiting for the manuscript to arrive, from Ellen Coleman to Karen Hansen to Susan McDermott. My ever-supportive agent, Bert Holtje.

ABOUT THE AUTHOR

Jean Marie Stine has presented seminars on business writing, speed learning, and multiplying brain power throughout the U.S. She is the author of a number of non-fiction books, including *It's All in Your Head: Amazing Facts About the Human Mind* and *Writing Self-Help/How-To Books.* Her critically-acclaimed novel, *Season of the Witch,* was recently made into a motion picture entitled *Synapse.* Jean Marie currently lives in the Boston area, where she serves as Director of Publications at the International Foundation for Gender Education.

INTRODUCTION

Doubling your brain power begins here. Before you read any further, make a special note of the time. Now, continue reading at your accustomed rate.

Wish you were smarter, could think quicker, remember better, read faster, comprehend new things readily? You can! Lying untapped in your brain are incalculable mental resources. By applying new scientific discoveries and insights into the mind, you can put that unused brainpower to work for you.

This book provides a step-by-step program for doing just that and literally doubling your brain power. By simply making greater use of mental capacities you normally take for granted, you will develop the ability to

❐ Cram hours of study into 30 minutes—or less.

❐ Master new job skills instantly.

❐ Become an expert on any subject in a single evening.

❐ Glean all you want to know from piles of documents in minutes by reading smarter.

❐ Remember word for word every key statement that is made by a speaker.

❐ Zip through complicated reports in minutes.

❐ Spot bogus information and hidden biases instantly.

❐ Understand what you learn better than those who plod word by word.

❐ Evaluate information and put it to practical use—instantaneously.

In every chapter of this book, you will discover easy-to-use, scientifically based tools guaranteed to double your brain power. In this introduction alone you will find nine techniques and strategies. Altogether, you will find more than 66 Brain Power Doublers—hints, techniques, exercises, and strategies—that you can use to boost your mental efficiency. If you make use of even 10 percent of these, you will leap lightyears beyond others in your ability to comprehend and respond to any and every mental challenge.

TAPPING YOUR BODY'S OWN NATURAL MIND MAXIMIZERS

You don't have to wait until later to put these Brain Power Doublers to the test. You can experience their marvelous potency for yourself— right now. Following you will find six strategies for boosting your mental abilities that don't require learning a single technique, step, or rule. They maximize brain power by making strategic use of recent scientific discoveries about the body and mental efficiency.

1. *Mental acuity:* When challenges require you to operate at your mental best, learn to notice and take advantage of the hour out of every hour and a half when your conscious mind functions at its optimum (you can usually sense when it begins to run down and get sluggish).

2. *Problem solving and inspiration:* When you are challenged for a solution or are seeking creative insight, try it during the half hour out of every hour and a half when your conscious mind slows down and your unconscious swims nearer the surface (you can usually sense this state coming on; you feel drowsy and your conscious thoughts begin to wander and slow down).

3. *Overall mental functioning:* For a lasting mental boost, exercise 12 minutes each day (those who do experience a 30-percent increase in brain power).

4. *Short-term memory:* When you have something you want to commit to your short-term memory, do it in the morning (the part of your brain that stores short-term memory is about 15 percent more efficient in the morning).

5. *Long-term memory:* When it's something you want to store in your long-term memory, do it in the afternoon (that portion of your memory bank reaches its peak in the afternoon).

6. *Recalling important facts and figures:* When you must remember key information for a meeting or test, review it first and then sleep on it (those who do typically experience 20 to 30 percent better recall).

DOUBLING YOUR BRAIN POWER IS A NECESSITY

These days doubling your brain power isn't a trick, it's a necessity. In our competitive, high tech, information-intensive society, brain power is the key to professional and personal achievement.

And the pace—quick as it is now—will only pick up over the next few years as we enter the twenty-first century. Already new technologies and new information processing and delivery systems—along with the new job skills they will require and the new areas of employment they will open up—are in the wings, waiting to be released. These will take us far beyond the CD-ROM, PC, and cable television industry just as they took us from cumbersome encyclopedias, the typewriter, and local television broadcast stations. And already scientists are at work on the generation of advances beyond them.

Today, as never before, there is compelling need for increased brain power, as business consultant Everette Dennis points out. Clearly there will be better job and financial opportunities. But other high stakes will also be missed by people who fail to make the fullest possible use of their mental resources.

Without the ability, for example, to constantly learn new job skills *throughout your life,* you will be left in the dust of the emerging new technologies. You may have thought learning and study ended with college. The truth is that you will be required to learn up to ten times as much after you graduate as you learned in college just to do and keep your job.

Soon, Dennis says, "everyone will find it necessary to recycle back through school after more than ten years. In particular, fast-moving technological skills will become obsolete every five years or so."

On the personal level, there are decisions about how we spend our money, and about our safety, family, politics, friends, and leisure time. For these to be informed choices, we have to absorb and evaluate a bombardment of information from television, radio, sales presentations, self-improvement courses, relationship-strengthening seminars, and a host of other media. In the twenty-first century, these choices and what we must know to make them can grow only more complex.

Yet the approaches we were taught in school to putting your brain power to work on these problems are more than three thousand years old. Worse, they are painfully slow, never worked well for many people, and are hopelessly inadequate for assimilating the amount of information the average adult is called on to master every day: classes, lectures, presentations, reports, meetings, names, dates, facts, figures, altered procedures, and more.

Fortunately, many of the same sciences that have created these challenges have also shown us the way to meet them. Thanks to researchers, we now know how to think smarter, learn smarter, remember smarter, read smarter, and listen smarter. Breakthroughs in our understanding of how the mind works have blueprinted methods anyone can take advantage of to develop their mental capacities. With vastly improved brain power, you will not only keep up with the demands of the twenty-first century—you will actually get ahead.

SCIENTIFIC TECHNIQUES THAT BOOST MENTAL ABILITY

Over the past two decades, scientific inquiry into the brain has produced breathtaking results. New ways of tapping and focusing its innate abilities have been made, virtually unnoticed, in every field of biological and psychological research. The implications of these discoveries for the average person are incalculable. Applied correctly, these new scientific insights into the functioning of the mind can help you double and even triple your brain power.

By applying these breakthrough discoveries, it's possible to enormously multiply

❐ Your learning power.

❐ Your memory power.

❐ Your reading power.

❐ Your listening power.

❐ Your thinking power.

All this may sound too good to be true. But science really has uncovered methods that will do all that for you—and more. For example, research shows that *within one hour, 60 percent of all we learn is forgotten—80 percent within one month!* One scientific formula you'll pick up in this book (Chapter 5) takes advantage of *a natural learning cycle that enables you to retain up to 90 percent of everything* you need to remember for years! Here's another example: Most of us have been taught such poor reading habits that you *can double your reading speed just by reading smarter—without using a single speed-reading technique* (when speed-reading methods are added, reading rates can easily double again).

DOUBLING YOUR BRAIN POWER TAKES NO ADDITIONAL EFFORT

Incredible as it may seem, it's true. When you know the simple scientific short-cuts, using twice as much of your mind doesn't take twice as much effort. You simply learn to use your brain more efficiently, producing double the result with no more mental energy than before

According to experiments by Allan Givens, director of EEG Systems Laboratory, it takes as much energy to scribble mindlessly as to paint a masterpiece. Gevins used an eight-channel EEG to record the brain waves of artists engaged in serious drawing and people who were just doodling. He thought artists who were concentrating would generate more mental energy than did the doodlers.

To his surprise, Gevins found no difference in the amount of brain power either group used. He concluded that it takes no more mental energy to create a masterpiece than most of us use on a typical day. The moral is clear: Since you have to generate just as much energy to goof off as to paint a masterpiece, you might as well paint a masterpiece.

ANYONE CAN DOUBLE HIS OR HER BRAIN POWER

Take Gary V., one of my workshop students. Gary had degrees in communication and media and was the editor-in-chief of a major metropolitan newspaper. If anyone should have felt he had brain power to spare, it was Gary.

Yet he confessed to me over lunch that "I feel stupid. It's like I'm drowning in information. It crosses my desk in a never-ending flood: circulation figures, advertising revenues, hundreds of key news stories to follow, meetings, sales presentations, correspondence, print-outs—you name it. Then at night, there's all the other stuff I should read: important articles, clippings, new books I want to read, new books I have to read. Why can't I absorb it all? Instead, I store it, I put it away I never get around to most of it. Worse, I end up feeling frustrated, inadequate, and guilty."

Sound familiar? Does this strike a chord? If so, like Gary V., you'll never feel that way again.

Before we reached dessert, I taught Gary a brain power doubler you'll find later in this book. Using it allowed him to zero in on and permanently retain the 10 percent of his daily information quota that was actually relevant, while bypassing the rest.

He called me back a week later to report that the technique had worked. "I can pay better attention to the parts that are important because I no longer feel obligated to try and pay attention to everything." As a result, Gary claimed he felt twice as smart. He also felt less pressured during working hours, had no trouble getting through his nighttime reading, and had also freed up additional time he could devote to other activities.

Gary was on his way to doubling his brain power. Using the same mental shortcuts (Chapter 8), you, too, can boost your brain power 100 percent or more when it comes to reading and absorbing piles of printed information.

WHY YOUR BRAIN IS MORE POWERFUL THAN A COMPUTER

Have trouble believing all this? Then consider: You have no doubt about the ability of the home computer to instantly "learn" any new program fed into it, to instantly remember everything it's told, read data from other sources instantly and effortlessly, or instantly to sort and retrieve stored data on demand.

Yet computer scientists say they are many generations away from being able to build a computer that will equal the complexity, storage, retrieval, or sorting capacities of the human brain.

You've got a whole lot more to work with than the world's most powerful computer. That means you can do anything a computer can do—faster and better.

Still not convinced? Don't worry. Most people who learn about my mental doubling techniques are the same way.

They are enticed, even excited by the idea of doubling their brain power. They are even willing to believe that I and others have developed computerlike minds and doubled our brain power. But they don't believe that they can do it.

There are two main reasons why most people don't believe they can double their brain power. The first is that it runs counter to what they have been taught to believe about the capacities of the human mind. The second is that they have had negative experiences in school or in other traditional learning environments (seminars, workshops, lectures, and so forth) that have given them a poor impression of their own brain power.

But science has overturned traditional views of how the brain functions and especially how it functions best. In the process, they have developed many powerful learning processes you can use, almost like software, to access your own brain's computer powers, gaining the capacity almost instantly to learn, read, evaluate, act on, and remember whatever is thrown your way.

THE OTHER 90 PERCENT OF YOUR BRAIN

You may have heard it said that we humans typically use only 10 percent of our brain, that the other 90 percent goes unused. This is a misconception. The unused portion is actually closer to 99 percent.

That means most of us typically make use of only 1 percent of our brain power.

Consider the following questions posed by these scientific facts about our mental capacities, as quoted in *The Brain* by the late Professor Isaac Asimov:

❐ Why aren't we better learners, when we have 200 billion brain cells? (That's as many stars as there are in some galaxies.)

☐ Why aren't we better at remembering, when our brains are capable of retaining about 100 billion bits of information? (That's the equivalent of 500 encyclopedias.)

☐ Why aren't we faster thinkers, when our thoughts travel at more than 300 miles per hour? (That's faster than the fastest bullet train.)

☐ Why aren't we better at understanding, when our brains have over 100 trillion possible connections? (That puts the most sophisticated computer to shame.)

☐ Why aren't we more creative, when we average 4,000 thoughts every 24 hours. (That's 40 dollars a day at a penny per thought.)

The answer is simple. Most of us habitually access a minute fraction of our brain power. About 10 percent, say scientists at the Sanford Research Institute. That leaves 90 percent of your potential brain power untapped.

"Turn up the gain" a bit—access say just 20 percent of your total brain power—and you double the amount you are currently using. Switch your mind all the way on—use all its talents and capabilities, all of the time—and you multiply it a hundredfold.

This isn't a pie-in-the-sky promise. Science has shown how to do that.

This book gives you breaking-edge scientific strategies, techniques, and mental shortcuts, many fresh out of the laboratory, that will enable you to "upgrade" the efficiency, complexity, and power of your mind in almost every arena.

DOUBLE YOUR MEMORY POWER RIGHT NOW

When these scoffers ask for "an example," I tell them about "Memory Glue." Memory Glue is a way of using certain innate capacities of the mind for remembering what you need to remember when you need to remember it.

One scoffer, Maria S., was an assistant to the lieutenant governor of the state. After many disillusioning experiences in politics, she was a hard-headed woman who was not about to believe anything that wasn't proven to her personal satisfaction. I described the six-step Brain Power Doubler I call "Memory Glue." This technique literally turns your brain into mental "flypaper" for important facts and figures. Maria laughed. It couldn't be that simple, she said.

Yet she called me the next afternoon to inform me that she had tried using the Memory Glue technique when she was deputized to report the details of a long, complex forestry reclamation meeting to the governor. Memory Glue had turned the trick, more than doubling her memory power. Maria had been able to recite every key point from memory. Soon I found her enrolled in one of my workshops.

BRAIN POWER DOUBLER

Next time you have something important to remember, try affixing it firmly to your mind with Memory Glue. Just follow these six simple steps.

1. Believe you will remember it (this focuses the whole brain on the effort).

2. Will yourself to remember it (this activates internal brain modules for remembering).

3. Visualize—or repeat once—clearly in your mind whatever it is you want to remember (this brings the material before the focus of your whole mind, conscious and unconscious, and directs it straight to the correct memory modules).

4. Consciously tell yourself to remember it (this extra force works like a hypnotic or programming command that will actually make the unconscious mark the information as extra special, making it stand out more vividly for easy retrieval).

5. Mentally review what you wanted to remember the next morning.

6. Review the material (this refreshes the memory, auto-corrects discrepancies, and reinforces it further).

THE MOST POWERFUL BRAIN POWER DOUBLER OF ALL

It may be hard to believe, but just paying attention can double your brain power. In a sense, this system underlies all the other memory doublers science has developed.

Whether you are awake or asleep, at any given moment, 24 hours a day, 7 days a week, millions of your brain cells are at work. Even when you are asleep, your brain is constantly sending and receiving information on the position of your limbs, the temperature of your body, and all the thousands of individual activities involved in breathing, digesting, dreaming.

But, typically, how aware of all this are you? How much advantage do you take of it? How much attention do you pay to what is going on around you?

According to a University of Minnesota survey conducted by psychologist Eric Klinger, Ph.D., we concentrate on what we're doing only about a third of the time. Most of our attention is occupied with relationships, personal problems, and people who have made us angry. Rather than focusing on matters at hand, on a typical day we spend our time this way:

❏ Thirty-three percent concentrating on current surroundings or activities

❏ Twenty-five percent thinking about others and interpersonal relationships

❏ Six percent actively thinking and problem solving

❏ Three percent considering self-praise or self-criticism

❏ Three percent worrying about things that make us anxious

❏ Two percent giving self-instruction

❏ One percent thinking about committing violence

❏ The remaining 26 percent of our daily thoughts are scattered among a wide variety of subjects.

You can see that by eliminating just some of this scattered thinking, it is possible to tap into twice as much of the data your brain is absorbing. Eliminating all divergent thinking would provide complete access.

It's true. Concentration alone can double your brain power. Experiments at the University of California in San Diego proved the old adage: You can't do two things at once—at least not well. When you split your attention, you cut your potential brain power in half.

In an experiment, people were asked to label items on a list with the right hand while pushing a button with their left every time they heard a certain note in a series of musical tones. The results showed the dramatic decline of mental ability when their concentration was divided. Test subjects always pushed the button more slowly when the tone came while they were writing labels. They were also more likely to make a mistake on the label when they were pushing the button.

Brain Power Doubler

You can put these University of California findings to work in your life right now. You'll discover an expanded version of this exercise in Chapter 8.

1. Look at a clock or watch.

2. Note how long it has taken you to read the past few pages.

3. Now return to reading. This time, make a conscious effort to concentrate on reading as fast as you can without skipping anything.

4. (The fourth step is given at the end of this Introduction. Do *not* skip ahead and read it!)

YOUR BRAIN'S SECRET POWERHOUSE

Just as 90 percent and more of what goes on in a computer—millions of computations and operations per second—takes place off screen, so 90 percent of our mental activity takes place outside our conscious awareness. There in the unconscious are thousands of "mental modules . . . hardwired in the nervous system," writes clinical psychologist John F. Kihlstrom.

Our unconscious pretty much automatically runs such activities as eating, breathing, movement, language, visual perception, and myriad other processes of our minds and bodies for us. This mental powerhouse also monitors our body for signs of illness and disease; scans our minds for conflict and distress; assesses our environment for danger and threats; and relays and interprets perceptions, sensations, and feelings. Last, but by no means least, it is the repository of our memory, experience, and decisions—everything that makes us us.

Your unconscious is a mental powerhouse in many ways. For one thing, it's a lot smarter than your conscious, according to research by psychologist Pawel Lewicki. In one experiment, he had volunteers push buttons trying to guess where an *X* would appear next on a computer screen. Although it seemed random, the *X* was actually following a complex pattern, determined by ten interacting rules. Lewicki offered a $100 reward to anyone who could consciously figure out the rules.

But no one collected, although several of the volunteers tried. Yet, as they continued to play the game, all the students' response times quickened, and they began "instinctively" to choose the spot where the *X* would appear. Your unconscious, Lewicki concluded, is smarter than your conscious.

The Einsteins, Edisons, and Madam Curies were not that much—if any—smarter than the average person, says psychology professor Dean Simonton, Ph.D. Simonton, who has conducted many studies of intelligence and creativity, found there was no relationship between IQ and creativity. Most of the celebrated minds of history, Simonton believes, simply made better use of their unconscious mental powerhouse.

These geniuses, says psychologist Earnest Rossi, Ph.D., get their ideas from the same place everyone else gets them—the unconscious mind. "It is now well established that the unconscious mind is the well-spring of all human creativity," Rossi writes. We all have moments when "creative ideas or insights bubble up into consciousness from their source in the unconscious," Rossi continues, "when we grasp the solution to a vexing problem, suddenly have a new perspective, or are hit with a flash of inspiration."

Like Lewicki's students, Einstein, and Beethoven, your unconscious is a mental genius. They unknowingly set that genius to work for them when they tapped into their unconscious mental powerhouse blindly, by instinct. You can learn to do it consciously, using the ideas in this book to greatly multiply your own brain power and freeing the genius hidden in the other 90 percent of your brain.

BRAIN POWER DOUBLER

Next time you are stuck for an idea or desperately need insight into a problem, this potent visualization exercise will lead you to the answers. It uses images (the language of the unconscious) to help you access the powers of your own unconscious mind.

1. Sit down quietly where you will not be interrupted.

2. Close your eyes.

3. Imagine that you are walking through a forest. (Take the time to build up a vivid image of the forest around you. Try to see, smell, and feel it as completely as you can.)

4. Now imagine you have come to a rustic house. (Again, try to build up a detailed image of the house, windows, door, roof, the grounds that surround it.)

5. Mentally open the door and step inside.

6. Visualize a wise old person standing in the middle of the room. Visualize her or him as fully as possible. Tell that wise old person your problem.

7. Listen closely to what you imagine he or she would say.

THE KEY IS IN YOUR HANDS

Applying the techniques in this book will transform your life. If you utilize even one idea from each chapter, you will be far better prepared not just to survive but to excel when faced by the challenges and opportunities that the twenty-first century will bring. Just making use of the six natural mind maximizers and the three Brain Power Doublers you've already learned will give you an enormous boost along the road to professional and personal achievement.

Ultimately, the choice is yours. I can put the key in the lock, but you have to turn it. I can give you simple, easy-to-acquire tools that will enable you to double your brain power. But I can't learn to use them for you. You have do that.

In today's world, you have only two choices: Stay as you are and continue to be overwhelmed by its demand for ever newer skills, ever increased learning, ever mounting performance ratings. Or take advantage of the unprecedented new discoveries about the mind and the learning technologies they have spawned to put all the assets of your mind to work all of the time.

The key is in your hands. The decision is yours.

Note the time. Calculate how long it has taken you to finish the last few pages while concentrating harder on reading. Compare that with your time for the previous group of pages (the number of words is about equal). Notice how much faster you were able to read just by concentrating on it a little harder. See what a difference just concentrating can make in your brain power? Convinced? Then read further.

CONTENTS

―――――――――――――― PART I ――――――――――――――

DOUBLING YOUR LEARNING POWER

Chapter 1
INSTANT LEARNING / 29

Chapter 2
TAPPING YOUR "OPTIMUM" LEARNING STATE / 43

Chapter 3
DISCOVERING YOUR PERSONAL LEARNING STYLE / 55

Chapter 4
MASTERING THREE STAGES OF LEARNING / 69

PART II
DOUBLING YOUR MEMORY POWER

Chapter 5
INSTANT MEMORY / 79

Chapter 6
POWER MEMORY—USING MNEMONIC TECHNIQUES / 87

Chapter 7
MEMORY MAPS—THE POWER OF PERSONALIZING / 97

PART III

DOUBLING YOUR READING POWER

PART IV

DOUBLING YOUR LISTENING POWER

I

DOUBLING YOUR
LEARNING POWER

Chapter 1

INSTANT LEARNING

In the course of the average day, we are called on to exercise all our mental abilities. Changes in employment, software, equipment, or personal interests require us to learn new skills. Newspapers, reports, faxes, e-mail, and textbooks all contain information that must be read for job and personal advancement. Bosses, instructors, co-workers, television news anchors, friends, and family tell us vital information we must listen to carefully. From every side our memories are tested with a wealth of facts we must remember. And whether it's the office, the classroom, or home life, there are dozens—if not hundreds—of professional and personal problems for us to think about.

Every day, in every aspect of our lives, we must draw on every one of our brain's abilities to keep up with the swiftly moving world around us. And most of us feel we aren't making it, that our mental powers aren't sufficient to meet the demands career, education, and family place upon them. How many times have you wished you had more of one brain power or another, in the wake of a situation in which you felt your own didn't measure up?

And if you could choose to double any one of your mental abilities, which brain power would it be? What do you think is the single most important of your mental abilities? Would you rather be able to

- ❏ Remember better?
- ❏ Read better?
- ❏ Listen better?
- ❏ Think better?
- ❏ Learn better?

Now, review the list again. Ask yourself which of the five you feel it would be the most difficult to change and improve?

Whatever your answers, glance over the list a final time. One of those five choices encompasses the other four. Double it and you automatically double your performance in the rest. Can you tell which it is?

The answer is learning. Double your ability to learn and you automatically double your brain power. If you answered "listen better," why did you want to listen better? Because you wanted to remember what you heard better. And why did you want to remember it better? So you could make better use of it. And what does making better use of what you hear come down to? Learning from it.

Learning power may be the most fundamental form of brain power. It is even more fundamental than thinking power. No matter how brilliant you were—if you couldn't learn anything—all that brain power would be wasted. But even if you were pretty dim—as long as you could learn—you'd have plenty of brain power to spare.

Goose up your learning power and you automatically goose up your brain power. The same is true of reading and remembering. A boost in your learning power means a boost in all three. If you could learn better, you could learn to read better, remember better, even think better.

Yet of these five, most people are convinced learning is the single hardest to improve. They believe that it's possible for them to listen more carefully, read faster, remember more accurately, and think more effectively. But they are equally passionate in their conviction that learning is an innate ability that can't be improved; either you are born a good learner or you aren't.

People feel that they were born inferior learners and that is that. Like height or the ability to play the violin beautifully, nothing can be done about it. They believe, in short, that you can't learn to be a better learner.

You probably believe the same thing about yourself and learning. In fact, millions of—perhaps most—people feel this way. They share an absolute conviction that they are among those unfortunates born among the slowest learners, and that almost everyone else is better at learning. It's likely you feel this way too.

The irony is that the very people we think are better learners than ourselves consider themselves poor learners, and think we are better at it than they are. Clearly, there is something wrong with this picture. In fact, there are several things wrong with it. That's because it is based on a number of *incorrect assumptions* about learning.

The first is thinking that you are a lousy learner. The majority of us suffer from this illusion in part due to the antiquated—and worse—counterproductive way of learning our educational system drilled into us as children. This old-fashioned approach actually does more harm than good and makes learning harder for us, not easier.

The school system taught, and still teaches, children to memorize data by rote. They are required to repeat names, dates, and facts over and over hundreds of times, until they are engraved in their memories. And that's all we are ever taught about learning.

This system never worked well in the first place. Most of us had trouble remembering half of what we had learned by the end of the week. By the time we become adults, more than 99 percent of it was forgotten.

The absurdity of leaving people to rely on the same cumbersome system to carry them through high school, college, and beyond into life and the workplace is obvious. Just think of everything you have to learn in a single day. Now imagine trying to learn it all by repeating each fact over a few dozen to a few hundred times. You couldn't get through it all in the average week, which explains a lot about your sense of being overwhelmed by the flood of information in your life.

As far as the educational system—and most of our learning skills—goes, the last hundred years of research into how we acquire and retain information might never have happened. In consequence, we internalize a primitive and inadequate approach to learning that typically proves inadequate to almost every learning challenge. It is slow, hinders rather than facilitates acquiring knowledge, and makes learning up to 100 percent more work than it needs to be.

Because we were not taught to learn effectively, we struggle to develop skills and vital knowledge, only to discover we have absorbed a tenth or less of what we needed to know. Because we were not taught to remember effectively, we forget key material on tests and at meetings. We were not taught to read effectively; therefore we find plowing through books, magazines, and reports painful, slow, and unproductive. We also were not taught to listen effectively, so we find all that we have heard slipping through our mental fingers like sand through a sieve after lectures and briefings. And because we were not taught to think effectively, we blunder down dead ends, draw wrong conclusions, and always seem to be one step behind the rest of the world.

Another reason we think just about everyone else is a better learner is that we are always present during our learning disasters. So we become only too aware of what we consider our failings. But since we are rarely present at or aware of other people's shortcomings in the acquisition of knowledge, we assume they must have superior overall ability when it comes to learning.

No wonder we think of learning as difficult, burdensome, a great deal of effort, and ourselves as class dunces. To most of us, the idea of learning conjures up the image of a difficult, laborious, and very tiring task, one we, personally, are not good at. The odds are you have a similar negative response to the thought of having to learn something new.

But scientists like Mihaly Csikszentmihalyi have proved anyone—and that includes you—can be an instant learner. You already have all the critical abilities. They're hardwired into your brain. For instance, research shows it takes only one tenth of a second for us to understand the spoken or printed word. All you lack is the skills—the mental tools—learning researchers have been discovering over the last three decades.

How would you feel about learning, and yourself as a learner, if you could be an instant learner? What if acquiring knowledge were instantaneous and effortless? What if you had only to hear a fact, read a report, or see a demonstration once to learn it forever?

With skills like these, you'd never again view yourself as a poor learner and face every situation requiring learning as a dull, difficult task. You'd probably consider yourself a learning wiz and look forward to learning as an exciting opportunity to display your mastery while adding to an ever-growing fund of knowledge. What's certain is that effective learning skills would give you an unexcelled edge when it comes to learning over most of those around you; and you'd easily stay on top of and get ahead of every report, class, and seminar you needed to know in your career or private life.

In fact, even without these skills, you were born with such natural gifts for learning that you are probably already a terrific learner without realizing it. Even with all the handicaps of attempting to learn with the primitive set of techniques taught in elementary school, you have already acquired a fabulous amount of learning ability during your lifetime. Now you are going to discover how to identify and draw on these abilities, while supplementing them with a whole set of cutting-edge learning techniques that will multiply your learning power many times over.

In this chapter, you will begin to pinpoint the learning skills you already have, overcome negative attitudes that impede learning, and take the first steps toward making it a pleasurable experience you'll find yourself looking forward to.

YOU ARE ALREADY A FABULOUS LEARNER

Have any of these scenarios ever happened to you?

- ❐ Your boss calls you in and hands you a complex manual of new protocols you are going to have to learn now that the entire company is using a new software system.

- ❐ Due to a delivery snafu, 200+ pages of crucial specs hit your desk at 4:30 P.M., and you will be expected to discuss even the smallest details knowledgeably in a transatlantic phone conference the next morning.

- ❐ You marry into a family with very different traditions and want to learn them and "fit in" as quickly as possibly because you love your spouse.

- ❐ You come home from your first evening in a real estate course with an intimidating, inches-thick textbook and realize you are expected to absorb it in just six weeks.

- ❐ A change in your life situation suddenly forces you to learn to drive a completely new kind of vehicle.

- ❐ To get a promotion, you attend a lecture on a subject you must master and find yourself faced with the most boring speaker in the world.

Most people have found themselves in situations such as these. And their reactions were pretty much the same. They felt intimidated, questioned their own adequacy, and doubted their ability to successfully learn it all.

The odds are you have a similar negative response to the thought of having to learn something new. To most of us, the idea of learning conjures up the image of a difficult, laborious, tiring task, one we are not very good at.

All humans are natural learners; it is part of our heritage. But most of us do not realize this for two reasons:

❑ Negative learning experiences in (and outside) the educational system

❑ Lack of any training in how to apply often unsuspected natural learning talents to learning

Have trouble believing you are such a great learner? Convinced you are a poor learner—one who absorbs new things slowly and only with great difficulty?

That's because, if you're like most people, you tend to focus on the times you've had trouble learning (through the use of archaic, ineffective learning techniques you're about to replace with effective ones). You probably rarely—I'm willing to bet never—stop to think of what you have already learned in life and all that you learn every day.

You learned to walk—no mean feat—using hundreds of subtle movements and placements of muscle, weight, balance, and momentum. You learned to talk—another truly amazing accomplishment you can be proud of—using thousands of words and dozens of complex rules (all of which you have down so pat they mesh flawlessly every time you open your mouth to speak). You also learned to read, write, add, subtract, multiply, and divide; you learned a fair smattering of history, geography, science, politics, and maybe a language or two; and you probably learned a lot about your favorite passions, whether they are local charities, sports, movies, TV, antiques, automobiles, old coins, high fashion, golf, or sci-fi. Then there are the hundreds, perhaps thousands, of large and small details you had to learn about your job. And what about all the new "do this" and "do that," procedures, pick up this, meet so and so at ten thirty next Wednesday, and a whole lot more that you absorb (learn) every day, routinely, without ever realizing you are doing it or what a fabulous learner you are. The following exercise is designed to help you reconnect with your own native talents as a learner.

BRAIN POWER DOUBLER #1

Review the results of this exercise any time you begin to doubt your incredible learning abilities.

1. Take out a sheet of paper or open a computer file.

2. List some of the things you learned in school that you can still remember now.

3. List things you have learned in pursuit of leisure activities, hobbies, or sports.

4. List things you learned for your current job.

5. List them for previous jobs.

6. List other things you have learned unrelated to the above.

OVERCOMING THE FOUR BARRIERS TO INSTANT LEARNING

Elina R.'s supervisor couldn't understand her. They worked in the claims department of Allied/Amalgamated Insurance (not its real name). Elina was an excellent adjuster. She was also bright, energetic, ambitious, and really enjoyed the work.

As far as her supervisor was concerned, Elina seemed a prime candidate for a prestigious promotion to senior adjuster, accompanied by a hefty jump in salary. All she lacked were a few critical skills, and those she could easily acquire by taking a few night courses and attending a couple of company seminars.

But for some reason her supervisor couldn't fathom, Elina, who otherwise was an ambitious achiever, never seemed to be interested. Every time the supervisor raised the subject of acquiring the skills she needed for promotion, Elina would agree half-heartedly that it sounded like a great idea. But she would never actually act on the advice and enroll in any of the necessary classes or seminars.

Finally, Elina's supervisor couldn't stand it anymore. She had to know what the problem was, why Elina was so reluctant to take a few simple steps that would lead to a major promotion and raise. So she took Elina to lunch and asked her why she was so reluctant to move ahead.

Elina stopped in the middle of her quiche, turned bright red, and began to sputter. The fact was, Elina confessed, she did terribly in structured learning situations. She knew she was smart and could pick things up quickly by doing, but when it came to speeches, workshops, and courses, she flunked them over and over.

In fact, she hated them with a passion and looked ahead to the idea with dread. Unlike her usual focused self, Elina said, if she was in a lecture hall she went blank—she couldn't concentrate. Her attention wandered, and she had trouble remembering afterward what had been said.

Graded tests intimidated her, and she always did poorly on them. Though Elina could work quickly under pressure in an office, answers came slowly and with great difficulty—when they came at all—when she had to take a written test. And her performance reflected her mental turmoil.

Because of these failures, Elina explained, even the thought of taking a class or workshop made her sick. She wanted that promotion, but knew that if she had to take a class and do well, she would never get it.

Elina isn't alone. Millions of people are convinced they are poor learners and have the same unpleasant experiences with learning. Like Elina, they don't realize it, but their negative attitude is to a large degree responsible for the negative quality of their learning experiences.

The truth is that most of us could learn far more easily and faster than we do. But we prevent ourselves from learning. Our negative experiences in the educational system and social myths about learning convince many of us that we can't succeed anyway. When faced with forthcoming learning situations, we begin to program ourselves for stress and failure by mentally repeating a number of common negative misperceptions about learning. Among these negative self-statements are:

- ❑ "Learning is boring."

- ❑ "I'm not a good learner."

- ❑ "I can't learn" (or "I can't understand") "this subject."

- ❑ "I won't remember what I'm learning."

These messages are based on the premise that learning is a nearly impossible task we are doomed to fail. Repeating them to ourselves day in and day out generates anxiety whenever we have a report to read or a lecture to absorb. It also acts as a self-hypnotic report, programming the mind to shut down its learning centers just when we need them most. No wonder our learning outcomes so often match our learning expectations.

To change your learning outcomes from negative to positive, you'll need to reprogram your mind with positive messages about your abilities as a learner. This will be a lot easier now that you have a strong sense of your learning accomplishments from having worked through the preceding exercise. What motivational experts such as Neil Fiore, Ph.D., call "positive self-talk" is a powerful tool for mentally switching tracks so that we approach learning opportunities with energy and confidence, the mind's learning centers charged up and running at their optimum.

You'll find that the following system for reprogramming negative self-talk, adapted from Dr. Fiore's work, will quickly get you started linking your old negative attitudes toward learning in the positive direction of learning masters. Changing long-ingrained ways of thinking takes time, but you don't have to wait until you have completely stopped your negative thoughts to change your attitudes. Instead, you can use your awareness of the old self-talk pattern to alert you to switch your mental track to the language of the successful learner. Once you have done this several times, positive self-talk about learning will strengthen, becoming easier to initiate, while the old ones will atrophy.

For example, you sit down to review an article from a trade journal discussing important changes in the ways the world wide web is impacting your profession. The first thing you may notice is that your shoulders begin to droop forward in a depressed, burdened fashion. This is a clear signal that, even if you haven't heard yourself say "I'm not a good learner," your body is already responding to negative self-talk from deep inside your mind. At the moment you have that awareness, reverse its effects by counterprogramming your unconscious with the statement's opposite: "I am already a successful learner who has mastered many fields of knowledge during my life so far."

You can sense the power for positive transformation inherent in the latter statement. When you learn to catch yourself mentally in the midst of—or just before—negative self-talk about learning and replace it with its opposite, you set that power loose in the service of your own learning abilities. As you review the fallacies and damage in each of the following four negative statements, try to transform them into positive ones by taking the negative elements out and replacing them with positive elements.

"Learning Is Boring"

This cockeyed statement is the number one obstacle people place in their own path to learning. First, it's not true. Just reflect back and you'll recall many times when a learning opportunity felt exciting and you were so enthralled you lost track of yourself in it. But when you keep repeating that it's "boring" and make learning feel like an unappetizing time waster, it's hardly surprising that you feel restless and have trouble focusing your attention.

"I'm Not a Good Learner"

Athletes and business people use what is called "positive visualization" to ensure their success. According to peak-performance maven Charles Garfield, Ph.D., these people program their minds for victory by impressing images of themselves winning it. It may seem like mumbo-jumbo, but there is an impressive body of scientific documentation attesting to the technique's power to reprogram doubts or negative feelings, while reinforcing the unconscious belief in the ability to succeed. If dwelling on success can program you for success, imagine what constantly bombarding your mind with images of inadequacy and failure can do to set you up for failure. Keep repeating that you aren't good at something long enough and it becomes a self-fulfilling prophecy. Of course, you are a good learner or you could not be reading this book—you couldn't even afford to buy it.

"I Can't Learn" (or "Can't Understand") "This Subject"

This is another piece of errant nonsense. Learning about something you enjoy, such as African violets or the stats on every living Olympic figure skater, draw on the same mental abilities as learning the ins and outs of a new accounting system or the Japanese language. If you have learned one thing, you can learn another. But constantly telling yourself you can't learn Japanese will program the mental pathways involved in learning only to reject the information. It's like coating your fingers with oil before attempting to pick up a slick, smooth object. The mind will accept what you reiterate as fact, and whatever you hear or read on the subject will slide right off.

"I Won't Remember What I'm Learning"

If positive reinforcement can help you do things better, just imagine the effect of constantly telling yourself that you can't remember the details of a report. You are sending your brain the equivalent of a mental "erase" or "delete" command—one that wipes your mental files clean of the information just as fast as you fill them up.

Stop your mind from reiterating these destructive self-statements and replace them with self-talk that reinforces awareness of the power of your own natural learning capacities.

BRAIN POWER DOUBLER #2

When a learning opportunity begins to make you feel anxious, fearful, or stressed, use the exercise to counterprogram with a strong, positive belief in your ability to learn.

1. Reverse and rephrase your "Learning is boring" statement into its opposite. (Example: "Learning is exciting, involving, interesting.")

2. Reverse and rephrase your "I'm not a good learner" statement into its opposite. (Example: "I am an excellent learner who has already learned an extraordinary amount.")

3. Reverse and rephrase your "I can't learn" (or "I can't understand") "this subject" statement into its opposite. (Example: "I learned my job, English, math, and a lot about the world. I can learn this, too.")

4. Reverse and rephrase your "I won't remember what I'm learning" statement into its opposite. (Example: "I have already learned to remember many important things—names, facts, dates. I can—and will—remember the salient aspects of this.")

REWARD SUCCESSFUL LEARNING EXPERIENCES

Josiah was a manager of the old style. He made it clear from the start that employees had better measure up if they expected to keep their jobs. Those who made mistakes or performed poorly were summarily fired. People worked in a fearful, threatening environment, in anticipation of the penalties to come, their efforts focused on not making mistakes rather than on productivity or creativity.

Sinead was his opposite. She emphasized the rewards—employees who did well would receive raises, promotions, comp time, and bonuses. She openly praised in front of other employees those who did well. Her staff worked eagerly in an atmosphere of excitement, giving extra in anticipation of the benefits that lay ahead.

Which style of management do you think you would work best under? Which manager would you rather work for? If you are like most people, you probably picked Sinead. She was a practitioner of the "pull" approach to management. Josiah, on the other hand, was an advocate of the "push" or "punishment" school.

At one time there was much controversy over which system produced the best results. But scientific studies show the "pull" approach to be far superior. Companies, divisions, and departments using it consistently demonstrate higher company productivity, greater employee efficiency, and an enhanced bottom line.

What does all this have to do with learning? Even though most people would prefer to work under the "pull" method of management, they apply the "push" method to themselves when learning. As learning opportunities approach, these people attempt to urge themselves to greater achievement by dwelling on the disasters that will occur if they do poorly. They fill their minds with images of poor performance reports, bad grades, evaporated promotions, and of feeling stupid and worthless—a learning failure again.

It's hardly surprising that the idea of learning fills them with fear and trepidation. Using the "push" approach, all they can envision is the disastrous consequences that might result. The rewards and benefits of learning are not part of their mental picture.

They attempt to do everything they can to put off or avoid the seminar they have to attend or the demonstration video they need to watch. When the time comes to enter the classroom or turn on the video, they are so certain that the consequences will be personally disastrous and painful, they rush through the task with no real involvement or personal commitment. As a result, they grasp little of what they are supposed to learn, and the experience turns out as badly as they envisioned.

Don't make this mistake in your own life. If you've been trying to motivate yourself to learn with the "push" school, give "pull" a whirl. Shift your focus from disaster and punishment to benefits, rewards, and the exhilaration of mastering a new subject. You'll find you vastly increase your zest for learning, and that zest will in turn increase your ability to learn.

Brain Power Doubler #3

Over a period of time, the following structured program will create such strong, positive associations around learning that you will soon look forward with excitement to every opportunity.

1. When you know a learning opportunity is coming up, decide on a reward you will give yourself afterward, something you wouldn't ordinarily buy, do, or enjoy.

2. The more intimidated you feel, the more exceptional you should make the reward.

3. Mentally picture yourself enjoying the reward in as much detail as possible, how it would taste, feel, and be.

4. Any time you find yourself thinking about the learning opportunity, switch mental tracks and repeat step 3.

5. Repeat it immediately before the learning opportunity begins.

6. Any time during learning that you experience anxiety or other negative feelings, repeat step 3.

7. Afterward (no matter how things turned out), carry through on your promise and give yourself that reward.

Chapter 2

TAPPING YOUR "OPTIMUM" LEARNING STATE

The October 1966 *Magazine of Fantasy and Science Fiction* was a special issue focused on my late friend Isaac Asimov. Inside were three short stories, a science article, and a bit of doggerel by the biochemist, science writer, historian, and novelist. An editorial noted that Dr. Asimov, then 45, had written 75 books during the first 15 years of his career. It also commented, "If Asimov keeps going at the same rate he's maintained in the past 15 years, he'll have written some 225 books by the time he's seventy-five."

As much of the civilized world knows, this estimate was woefully inadequate. The ebullient Asimov went on to pen nearly 400 published books in even less time. Had he lived to 75, the total would have been closer to 450—double the original estimate.

What was Asimov's secret? Some have attributed it to an eidetic (photographic) memory. He did indeed have a good memory. But not a photographic one. Asimov makes frequent mention of his lapses in his autobiography, *In Memory Yet Green,* and admits he would have been unable to write it had he not kept a detailed diary of writing-related activities.

Asimov's ability to spew out such a gargantuan volume of erudition rested on his prodigious love of learning. He slurped down not merely books, but entire subjects. Asimov was no speed-reader, either. Instead, he possessed an enormous gusto for acquiring facts, figures, and fascinating data.

Asimov had to know about everything. He was consumed with an absolute passion to learn, an unending thirst to discover whatever there was to learn new and different in any situation or person. No matter what the circumstances, no matter whom he was with, no matter

43

whether he was reading or not, no matter how chance the acquaintance or boring the speaker—Isaac Asimov was always learning

How was an indifferent biochemist whose immigrant father had owned a candy shop in the Bronx able to become one of the twentieth century's most celebrated prodigies of learning? Was he born that way? Or is it something other people can learn?

The answer is simple: Asimov, like many other learning wizards, was able—whether consciously or unconsciously—to tap almost all the time into a natural mental state the rest of us enter only once in a while and by accident. In this state, we acquire information instantly, effortlessly, and with such delight that we want to keep on doing it until we drop.

You may doubt that you have ever had such an experience. But if you think back over your life, you doubtless recall at least one occasion when learning went exceptionally well for you, so well it still stands out vividly in your memory. It may have been a workshop, an illuminating book, an enthralling lecture, the day your father taught you fly-casting, or the time your mother taught you about the futures market. I call this your "Optimum Learning State." Others call it "peak performance," "the flow state," "the zone," and "the peak learning state."

Since the 1960s, scientists of many types have been studying the Optimum Learning State (OLS). University of Chicago researcher Mihaly Csikszentmihalyi has described it as "a state of concentration that amounts to absolute absorption in that marvelous feeling that you are in command of the present and performing at the peak of your ability." In the OLS, you are completely absorbed in what you are learning, and understanding is at a maximum.

Imagine what absorbing new ideas and information would be like if you could enter every learning situation in your OLS the way Asimov and other learning wizards do. Your brain power would be vastly multiplied. You wouldn't have to sweat that class in business writing, that new departmental flow chart, that new way of routing customer complaints, or that 200-page analysis of a competitor's bottom line anymore. You could master them with ease.

The good news is that you can. As the result of the work of Csikszentmihalyi and his colleagues, scientists have charted the OLS and the steps that lead to it. In the sections that follow, you will discover how to put their knowledge to use for you. By combining deep breathing, relaxation, and a few simple affirmations, you'll become able to enter the OLS any time you need to with a little advance preparation. You will also learn a special technique for retrieving information after any learning situation that caught you unprepared as if you had been in the OLS.

ACTIVATING YOUR OPTIMUM LEARNING STATE

Phillip was a chemistry major who came to me with a problem that perplexed him. On Tuesday, Phillip had attended a lecture on the Civil War in which he was not much interested. For some reason he couldn't comprehend, he had really "tuned in" on the speaker, seemed to understand every word the woman spoke, even anticipating her words. Phillip had felt unusually clearheaded, "really up," and experienced almost a letdown when the lecture ended. He had also done exceptionally in the pop quiz that followed.

Four days later, on Saturday, however, there had been a far more vital lecture on catalysts, a subject that had always fascinated Phillip and one he needed to make good marks in. The professor who spoke was a scintillating lecturer. Yet Phillip had felt mentally and physically "down," he couldn't seem to focus in on the lecturer, and when he did, he had trouble grasping what the man was saying; when he really made an effort to focus on the words, he still experienced difficulty understanding what they added up to. After the lecture, Phillip could barely recall anything the man said. Worse, he did poorly on the test that followed, one he desperately needed to pass.

Phillip lamented, "What's wrong with me?" If only I could have been 'on it' Saturday when it counted and not Tuesday when it didn't. If only I could just snap my fingers and be that good a learner all the time."

It wasn't the first time I have heard this story or that particular lament. On Tuesday, something had activated Phillip's Optimum Learning State. On Saturday, he was back to normal, and perhaps even a bit subnormal. We all enter OLS sometimes, at random moments, usually widely separated in our lives.

Chances are, you've had similar experiences. Of course, you didn't know they were called Optimum Learning States then; probably you had no word for them at all. And chances are you've ended up wondering what was "wrong" with you, wishing you too could "just snap your fingers" and recapture whatever set off the experience in the first place.

Now you can. The OLS doesn't have to be a random, sometime thing that comes and goes when it wants. You can enter the OLS whenever it's needed with only a little preparation. Research into optimum learning by Mihaly Csikszentmihalyi and others has pinpointed the combination of factors that trigger OLS. The result was a simple three-step technique that takes only a few minutes.

Earliest research into the Optimum Learning State linked them to theta waves. Investigations with EEG (brain wave) machines showed that when we are learning at our peak, our brains emit electromagnetic waves in the four-to-seven-cycles-per-second (CPS) or theta range. Most key states of consciousness from sleep to full consciousness produce their own characteristic brain waves.

Brain waves are usually ranked from the slowest to the fastest.

❑ Delta waves (1–3 CPS)—deep dreamless sleep

❑ Theta waves (4–7 CPS)—intense emotion or concentration

❑ Alpha waves (8–12 CPS)—relaxation and meditation

❑ Beta waves (18–40 CPS)—conscious awareness and dreams

The problem for those seeking access to the Optimum Learning State is that there is no known way for someone to deliberately trigger the theta waves (4–7 CPS). This stymied researchers for years. Then they noticed something interesting.

Theta waves associated with optimum learning and alpha waves associated with deep relaxation lie side by side, only 1 CPS apart. Normally, we think of intense creativity and quiet relaxation as completely different. But looked at in terms of their CPSs, it becomes obvious that the mental components in the deep relaxation state and the concentration state are closely related.

The key point here is that the theta wave learning state can't be brought on consciously, but the deep relaxation state can. The two states are separated by only a single cycle per second. This led me to the development of a three-step method for bringing the body and mind to the edge of the OLS and then slowing it down that all-vital one more cycle per second that activates the OLS itself.

Now, Phillip and all those like him can enter their OLS every time they need it and not just when it decides to "kick in" on its own. These three steps are

❏ Using deep breathing to create the OLS.

❏ Using relaxation to deepen the OLS.

❏ Using affirmation to lock in the OLS.

Using Deep Breathing to Create the OLS

Don't skip this if you want to double your brain power. There is no more important technique in this book or in any book. Deep breathing is the most fundamental factor involved in producing an OLS. If you've never tried it, you may dismiss the idea that anything as common, ordinary, and taken for granted as breathing can make you a kind of superlearner. It probably sounds like some kind of esoteric or mystical or soft-headed pseudoscientific nonsense. But there is a mountain of unimpeachable scientific evidence that deep breathing can create the conditions that underlie all optimum learning experiences. Breathing has such a potent effect on our minds because

❏ It soups up the amount of oxygen available to the brain, and the brain requires far more oxygen when it functions at peak learning levels.

❏ It relaxes the body and clears the mind of tension.

❏ It establishes a rhythmic physical cycle that attunes the brain to the 8–12 CPS alpha wave state.

In fact, like the deep relaxation exercise that follows Brain Power Doubler #7, deep breathing can give a healthy boost to your brain power when used just by itself.

BRAIN POWER DOUBLER #4

The following simple two-minute exercise can be used to help you prepare for learning a task or critical facts. Try it now and then continue to use it on a daily basis in the future.

BRAIN POWER DOUBLER #4 (cont'd)

1. Find a quiet place and sit comfortably, spine erect.

2. Put your right hand above your navel and your left hand just below the rib cage. Then relax your abdominal muscles.

3. Take an easy, natural breath. (Don't draw it in with your stomach muscles. Just let your lungs draw it in naturally. Your right hand should move slightly as a result of the inhalation, not from forcing it with your stomach muscles. At the same time, your chest will expand, causing your left hand to move outward and upward. Again, the movement should arise solely from your inhalation, not from your stomach muscles.

4. Exhale by reversing steps 1 and 2. (Let the air naturally flow out without forcing it.)

5. Practice this for a few minutes until you feel you have begun to breathe comfortably, naturally, easily.

6. Now begin to inhale slowly through your nose to a count of four. (Visualize the oxygen being drawn straight from your lungs to your brain.)

7. Hold the breath for a four count. (Visualize the oxygen cooling your brain.)

8. Exhale for a count of four. (Visualize any tensions in your mind or body being released with your breath.)

9. Repeat steps 5–7 five more times. (More could overoxygenate the brain.)

10. Resume natural breathing. By now you should be able to feel the shift away from ordinary consciousness and toward the alpha state.

Using Relaxation to Deepen Your OLS

Deep-breathing techniques can help quiet the mind while they energize the body and brain. They shift brain states from the 18–40 CPS beta waves of standard, everyday consciousness and closer to the 8–12 CPS of deep relaxation, which lie so near to the OLS.

But unless you deepen the alpha-wave relaxation state somehow, you'll lose it. Left to its own devices, your brain will quickly shift back up to the 18–40 CPS of daily consciousness. That's because your mind is designed to operate there, constantly surveying your environment and generating thoughts about it all the time.

According to studies by Jerome Singer, Ph.D., dean of consciousness researchers, no matter what else we are doing, our brains are wired to keep ticking along in thought—sorting information and generating possibilities, practical and impractical—through our every waking moment. When we have nothing else on our minds, this helps maximize the use of brain power that would otherwise be wasted. (Essentially, it's due to this little function that we moved from the cave to the condo and survived innumerable challenges along the way.)

Research by psychologist Eric Klinger, Ph.D., however, shows that when you are trying to learn, ordinary consciousness becomes an obstacle to the alpha state and the OLS just beyond. More than 75 percent of your learning power is drained off in "ticking along in thought—sorting information and generating possibilities." Klinger found that this left less than 25 percent of our brains free for acquiring new information and the task at hand.

It's possible to quiet those thoughts, deepening relaxation, releasing learning power, and moving closer to the OLS. The basic procedures have been well known for centuries and have recently been validated anew by scientists such as Herbert Benson, M.D., in research at Boston's Beth Israel Hospital. In the past, they went under names such as "prayer," "meditation," "yoga," and the "indwelling of the holy spirit."

Dr. Benson found that when he placed people in quiet, comfortable rooms and led them through a series of tranquil mental images, their brains soon began to produce alpha waves. As measured on his laboratory instruments, their minds became quiet, their breathing was measured, and they entered a state of deep relaxation. At the same time, their bloodstream became flooded with brain-boosting chemicals such as endorphins, benzodiazepines, and other neuropeptides that are released when we are happy, optimistic, and feel great.

Millions have used some variant of Dr. Benson's technique as a way of slowing their minds down to the 8–12 CPS of deep relaxation that serves as a gateway to the 7-CPS theta-wave state (Optimum Learning State).

Dr. Benson's approach produces a quiet, peaceful, alert mind and a deeply relaxed body and is amazingly easy to do. And as with deep breathing, the results on learning, writes Ronald Gross in *Peak Learning,* are "profound and beneficial" even when used on its own.

BRAIN POWER DOUBLER #5

When you have time to prepare for a few minutes before a learning opportunity, follow introductory deep breathing with this adaptation of Dr. Benson's approach to deep relaxation. They will bring you to the edge of the Optimum Learning State.

1. After a few minutes of deep breathing, close your eyes and begin breathing normally through your nose again.

2. When your breathing returns to ordinary, let yourself focus on the breath flowing quietly in and out from the tip of your nostrils.

3. If your attention starts to wander and distracting thoughts arise, don't hassle yourself over it; simply bring your attention back to your breathing until it begins to slow down or soften. (But don't consciously try to relax—just try quietly to observe.)

4. By now you should have reached the state of deep relaxation and mental quiet and be in the alpha state.

Using Affirmation to Deepen Your OLS

When breathing and relaxation have brought you to the edge of—or into—OLS, you can deepen it and shift yourself the rest of the way with affirmation.

An affirmation is simply an instruction you send your unconscious mind, much the same as you send one to your computer's CPU. Like the computer, the real work in your mind goes on out of sight, in the unconscious. You can't communicate with your unconscious directly, but you can communicate with it in its own special language, just as you do with a computer.

Affirmation is the mind's "programming language." It works because your subconscious is highly receptive to simple, positive statements. As Ron Gross writes, "Nowhere is this truer than in the realm of learning, because we are dealing with the state of our own minds, not external conditions."

What's important here is that affirmations have the power to program your mind to shift to the OLS, just as a computer command has the power to shift from one program to another. The OLS is a mental state, and mental states are particularly susceptible to affirmation. "I know," Gross says, "both from my own practice and from the experience of my students, that affirmations can work wonderfully in opening the mind [for] any learning experience."

Affirmations may "seem simplistic at first," Gross cautions, "but be patient; they have to be elementary to have an impact on our subconscious minds."

BRAIN POWER DOUBLER #6

Use these affirmations in conjunction with deep breathing and relaxation for a quantum leap into the OLS. But even repeated by themselves just before or during a learning opportunity will make you an optimum learner for the duration.

1. Repeat each of the following statements slowly and quietly to yourself one at a time.

2. Think about the meaning of each statement for a minute or so before moving on to the next.

3. After thinking about each, say it out loud once in a quiet, firm voice.

4. Here are the three statements that will open the gateway to the OLS for you:

"I am a terrific learner."
"I am entering the Optimum Learning State."
"I will learn easily and deeply."
"What I learn will interest and excite me."

5. Now, having boosted your brain power by shifting into the OLS, you can go out and make the most of your learning opportunity.

ACCESSING YOUR INNER "OPTIMUM LEARNER"

Does this experience sound familiar? You have been pondering a problem, unable to reach any solution, perhaps seeking a theme for your church's fund-raising efforts for the year. You are driving to the supermarket, thinking about something else, when suddenly you seem to hear someone speaking the solution in your ear or right beside you. "Religion's free—building maintenance isn't!"

Odds are, you've had more than one experience in which an ethereal voice produced just the phrase or forgotten datum or insight you needed in response to an urgent problem. According to creativity researcher Willis Harman, Ph.D., president of the Institute of Noetic Sciences, these experiences are common. But we are usually so caught up in the excitement of our sudden surge in brain power that we don't stop to think about the way in which it arrived. Or else, he adds, we accept the solution but try not to think about its source because it was just a bit weird.

This voice, says Harman, is our Inner Optimum Learner. Whether we are in an OLS or not, our unconscious is always in the optimum learning mode. It purrs along in the "flow" state, observing, remembering, comprehending, and drawing the correct conclusion from everything that takes place around it. Often we tap into it unwittingly, hearing what it has to say in the form of an ethereal inner voice.

When you haven't been able to enter the OLS before a learning experience, don't panic. All the knowledge is there just beneath the surface of consciousness in the guise of your Inner Optimum Learner. Harman has participated in research in which average people were taught to access their OLS via a deceptively simple visualization technique.

Don't dismiss the idea of tapping into your unconscious through visualization until you've given it a try. Imagining something vividly has a profound impact on the body and mind, Harman says, sending the same kinds of electrical signals down your neural pathways as real experiences. That's why the mouth puckers up when you think about biting into a lemon, or why we cry when we remember the death of a loved one, or we find our heartbeat slowing when we imagine the ebbing waves in a peaceful tropical lagoon.

The following approach to accessing your Inner Optimum Learner is adapted from Harman's *Higher Creativity,* written with co-author, Howard Rheingold.

BRAIN POWER DOUBLER #7

Whether it's a lecture, a report, or a meeting, here's how your Inner Optimum Learner can help you recapture anything and everything you feel your conscious self missed during the experience.

Brain Power Doubler #7 (cont'd)

1. Find a quiet, comfortable place to sit.

2. Take a few minutes to settle your mind and clear it of all distractions. (A simple prayer or mantra can help.)

3. Review your memories. Find a learning opportunity that went exceptionally well, one in which you felt "on it" all the way through the process and were "high" about it afterward.

4. Re-create the scene in your imagination as if you were viewing the scene and yourself (your Inner Optimum Learner) from above. Don't just try to "see" it. Build up a mental image of all the sights, sounds, and impressions you experienced there. Was it indoors or out? If others were present, try to picture their faces and hear their voices. Do your best to smell the smells, feel the feel.

5. Look down at yourself. Can you remember how you felt about what you were learning? Were you listening, reading, or performing intently? Was there a sensation of excitement, of strong fascination and interest?

6. Can you remember how you felt physically—healthy, in tune, alert? How you felt mentally—clear, unusually perceptive, mind following every detail as fast as quicksilver?

7. Can you remember how you felt about yourself as a learner, that you were doing well, that you were a good learner, that you were really on it?

8. Now imagine that you are floating down next to yourself in that learning situation. Ask that image of yourself (your Inner Optimum Learner) whatever it is you needed to know to have succeeded instead of failing. Make your question as specific as possible, whether it's the essential points, or something critical you have forgotten, or everything from the beginning. (You may want to take notes.)

9. Listen carefully to what your Inner Optimum Learner says. Try actually to hear the words. And don't hurry the process or interrupt. Give your Inner Optimum Learner plenty of time to answer.

10. When you are finished, relax, take a deep breath, and let it out before bringing the session to an end.

Chapter 3

DISCOVERING YOUR PERSONAL LEARNING STYLE

Have you ever known someone with his own unique style of doing things? Perhaps it was someone who did things exactly the opposite of how she was "supposed" to, but it worked for her? Most of us have had a friend or relative like that.

My friend José R. was like that. José owned a large hardware store in a small California town. Most of his employees had worked for him for years and had received raises accordingly. As a result they knew the store's stock by heart and could knowledgeably advise customers on the right screw or bracket or tool for any job.

Then one of those discount chain department stores moved into the area. You know the kind: run by Harvard MBAs on the bottom-line principle. They can offer a rock-bottom price because they hire teenaged clerks—without a clue about their jobs, the inventory, or the difference between a ring nut and a hazel nut—for minimum wage. People flock to these operations, where they often wander for hours in search of the few store personnel, attracted by the savings, putting local merchants—who can't compete with their price—out of business.

Most local merchants just keep on doing what they've always done, hoping customer loyalty will be stronger than the almighty dollar. It never is, of course, and eventually businesses that have been mainstays for decades—with a stake in the community, supporting local activities and charities, perhaps for generations—go under. Finally, the owner throws in the towel, a "for sale or lease" sign goes up on their building, and employees with many years of experience and knowledge are forced to take those minimum-wage jobs with the discount chains.

The few local merchants that do survive accomplish it by copying the discount chain's tactics: firing experienced employees, hiring minimum-wage know-nothing clerks, and getting their volume up by opening branches in other parts of town so they can order merchandise in large enough quantities to be able to offer competitive prices with the chain stores (in essence becoming mini-chains themselves).

José decided to take a completely different approach. He called all his employees together. He told them the situation he was facing. He didn't want to lower their pay or lay them off. On the other hand, it was obvious the discount store was going to siphon off all their customers and drive them out of business unless something was done.

José proposed the following to his employees: everyone's base pay would be tied to the store's pretax earnings. As long as it remained the same, so would their salaries. If it decreased, their pay would be decreased proportionally and vice-versa if it increased.

Everyone would work even harder to please customers and make them feel welcome. Store buyers would redouble their efforts to find quality overstocks and close-outs whose savings they could pass on to their customers. Sales personnel would work on increasing sales volume, helping lower costs and the price they had to charge customers.

Meanwhile, José would counter the chain's advertised "lowest prices in town," campaign with one emphasizing weekly specials, no 15-minute waits for a salesperson, and a knowledgeable and experienced staff that could help customers find the item they wanted—or the right item—almost instantly.

I wouldn't be telling you this story if José's strategy hadn't worked. His employees threw themselves totally behind the plan. Sales held even, then went up. As volume increased, José was able to lower prices even further. Within 18 months, the discount hardware chain threw in the towel and their fancy new warehouse-style building sold at distress prices to a plastic extrusion outfit.

José's approach to the situation was certainly unorthodox. But then José is a unique individual. He was smart enough to realize that what worked for others wasn't right for him and tried a different style of solving the problem.

The fact is, we're all unique individuals. And we all have our own unique style of doing some things, a way that works well for us. When we have difficulty absorbing new ideas, says Robert Smith, professor of psychology at Northwestern Illinois University, in his book *Learning How to Learn*, it's often because we are using the wrong kind of learning style for us. Some people, he found, acquire information best in absolute silence, others only when Beethoven (or the Beatles) is blaring loudly. Professor Smith's research at Northwestern Illinois led him to conclude that we all have a unique style of acquiring new knowledge.

According to Dr. Smith, we differ in how we go about key activities associated with learning. We differ in how we think and solve problems. We differ even in the manner we go about "information processing" (reaching decisions).

"With regard to method," Professor Smith writes, "one might hear a person say, 'I don't like discussion,' or, 'I went to a workshop and we did role playing—it made me uneasy.' With field trips we might hear, 'I fall behind and can't hear what the guide is saying.'"

Many of us, he points out, do best when we are told how to proceed at every point during the learning process. But there are an equal number who thrive only when we are offered less structure and more freedom of choice in such matters as what to study and where to begin. Most of us differ in the way factors such as competition, room temperature, background noise, and personal problems affect our absorbing of information.

Everyone, in short, possesses a distinctive personal style of acquiring acknowledge, a way he or she learns things fastest and best. We weren't taught this in school (to be fair, they didn't know it then). So most of us try to learn using that rigid, unwieldy system that was designed by others with no thought for individual needs or other equally valid ways of acquiring knowledge.

The result is inevitable. Trying to take in new information with an approach that doesn't match your own unique strengths and needs is like trying to swim upstream against a strong current: It's difficult, often impossible. No wonder so many of us come away from classes, seminars, lectures, and the like exhausted, discouraged, and convinced we are poor or slow learners at best.

But when you identify and apply your Personal Learning Style (PLS), acquiring knowledge is like swimming downstream: The speed of the current is added to your own swimming speed, multiplying your muscle power. Using your PLS multiplies your brain power; acquiring knowledge becomes effortless, almost instant.

The first three powerful exercises that follow boost brain power by helping you identify your own optimum ways of taking in new knowledge. The fourth shows you how to maximize knowledge of your optimum style, guaranteeing every learning experience is an optimum learning experience from now on.

DISCOVERING YOUR BEST LEARNING APPROACH

How well you learn depends on which end you start at. Researchers David Lewis and James Greene of London's Mind Potential Study Group have found that one aspect of our PLS has to do with how we best approach acquiring information. Half of us learn best, Lewis and Green say, when we approach a new subject "top down." The other half do best when we analyze it "bottom up."

According to Green and Lewis, top-down learners are people who

❏ start with a broad view.

❏ look for general principles, big ideas, basic concepts, and organizing principles.

❏ relate everything they know to the topic.

❏ are quick to draw parallels and notice relationships.

❏ prefer unstructured situations.

❏ like to jump right in to a subject.

❏ do poorly if data or skills are presented in a highly inflexible system.

Bottom-up learners are those who

❏ begin with facts.

❏ use a methodical, systematic approach.

❏ master each detail before moving on.

❏ have clearly defined goals.

❏ focus only on matters related directly to the subject at hand.

❏ do poorly in unstructured situations.

Top-down learners capture facts with amazing quickness when they begin with the big picture and then fit in the details. Bottom-up learners do the same thing if they can start with the details and build up to the big picture.

Things start to go wrong, however, when a top-down person given a computer manual starts with the details and plods through them one at a time. The poor top-down learner feels he or she is struggling to fit bits of random data together without having any overall idea of the picture they make or the idea they add up to. It's a sure setup for a negative learning outcome.

Or pity the bottom-up person given a chart of the general scheme of things designed by a top-down mind. To the bottom-up, it presents a vague, confusing picture of generalities but doesn't allow him or her to focus in on a solid foundation of detail. Bottom-ups won't have absorbed much afterward.

In both cases, it's the wrong approach for their particular learning style. It's a lot like AC and DC, or trying to fit a three-pronged plug into a two-pronged socket. But when top-downs get the chart of the overall situation or bottom-ups get the detailed, step-by-step computer manual, it's as if their learning power is being plugged in and hooked up to the right current. They begin to sizzle learningwise.

You probably have a pretty good idea by now of whether you are a top-down kind of person or a bottom-up individual. But do the next exercise anyway whether you do or not. It will help you determine which it is, if you are unsure. More important, it will help you begin to focus on the kinds of situations in which your personal approach could serve you best.

BRAIN POWER DOUBLER #8

Read through each of the pairs of phrases below. Place a checkmark next to the phrase that seems to express your own best way of approaching learning opportunities. Remember, there are no right or wrong answers. These descriptions are intended to help you focus more clearly on your own best approach.

1. When learning, do you
   a. [ ] like to collect data from several areas at once?
   b. [ ] like to focus on one area at a time?

2. When learning, do you
   a. [ ] like to acquire a little knowledge about every aspect of the subject?
   b. [ ] like to gain expertise in a single aspect?

BRAIN POWER DOUBLER #8 (cont'd)

3. When learning, do you
   a. [ ] like to know all kinds of interesting details about it, whether or not they are related to the subject at hand?
   b. [ ] like stick to "just the facts, ma'am"?

4. When learning, do you
   a. [ ] remember general principles best?
   b. [ ] remember specific facts best?

5. When learning from a manual or book, do you
   a. [ ] like to skip through, reading the sections that interest you most before reading the rest?
   b. [ ] like to read through one section at a time, in sequence, studying each item until you are certain you have fully assimilated it before moving on?

6. When you need information from someone else, do you
   a. [ ] like to ask about the bigger issues that give you the overall picture?
   b. [ ] like to ask very specific questions that give you a detailed grasp of the specifics?

7. When looking for something in a bookstore or library, do you
   a. [ ] wander from section to section, stopping to pick up any book that looks interesting along the way?
   b. [ ] go straight to the section devoted to the subject you're researching, select books from there, and leave?

8. When learning, do you
   a. [ ] like working only under general guidelines?
   b. [ ] like having detailed instructions?

If you placed a checkmark by five or more "a"s, you learn best from the top-down. If you checked five or more "b"s, you learn best from the bottom-up.

DISCOVERING YOUR BEST LEARNING SENSES

Do these situations sound familiar? DeFruscio in the stock room is better at putting things into words than most people. Allyson in accounting is always noticing the way things look. Tetsu in the computer department works well with others and is quick to sense their feelings as well. Miranda in telemarketing is very logical and can point out any flaws in any idea. Irving, who delivers from the deli down the street, is always humming or listening to music on headphones. Blanche, who works across the hall, is very in touch with herself and always knows what she is doing, what she feels, and why. Washington in marketing loves to ski, pump iron, play volleyball; and he moves with an almost balletic grace.

We all know people who relate better to words, or to what they see, or to what they hear, or to their bodies, or to logic and reason, or to other people—people who seem to take in the world better through one particular sense: hearing, seeing, feeling, or one of the rest. But we often fail to connect that knowledge to ourselves.

Yet studies by Harvard psychologist Howard Gardner show that using the right sense results in a remarkable rise in learning power. Someone whose best sense is hearing gets far more out of a lecture than does someone whose best sense is sight. Someone with strong inter-personal senses will get far more out of a role-playing exercise than will someone whose best sense is a logical mind. And likewise, someone whose best senses are kinesthetic will learn faster through hands-on doing than someone whose best senses are verbal.

Professor Gardner's research led him to conclude that there are seven learning senses. These are:

- ❐ Verbal
- ❐ Logical
- ❐ Visual
- ❐ Musical
- ❐ Kinesthetic (body movement)
- ❐ Intrapersonal (self-knowledge)
- ❐ Interpersonal (knowing others)

Have you ever thought about your own best sense or senses? Is it verbal, logical, visual, musical, kinesthetic, intrapersonal, or interpersonal? Or a combination thereof?

Now, apply that to acquiring a new skill or mastering new data. Chances are you'll recall that you learned fastest and retained it longest when the nature of the experience matched your best learning senses.

And you probably performed poorest in circumstances in which there was a strong mismatch.

Next time you are faced with a learning opportunity, don't take chances. Find a way of acquiring the information that allows you to make use of your best learning senses. The following checklist, adapted from Ronald Gross, will help you identify the senses through which you gather information most efficiently and identify how you can find ways to put them to use more often in the future.

BRAIN POWER DOUBLER #9

Figuring out your best learning senses isn't difficult. Simply place a checkmark by descriptions you feel apply strongly to you.

A. [ ] Do you find it easy to recall vivid turns of phrase or memorable quotes and use them in your own conversations?

B. [ ] Do you notice instantly when others are upset or troubled?

C. [ ] Are you fascinated by scientific and philosophical questions such as "Where did the universe come from?"

D. [ ] Do you quickly learn your way around new areas or neighborhoods?

E. [ ] Are you regarded as graceful and do you rarely feel awkward in your movements?

F. [ ] Can you sing on key?

G. [ ] Do you read articles and books on science and technology?

H. [ ] Do you notice wrong words and incorrect grammar when others use them?

I. [ ] Can you usually figure out how something works or how to fix something that's broken, without asking for help?

J. [ ] Do you find it easy to put yourself in other people's shoes and understand why they act the way they do (even if you refrain from commenting on it)?

K. [ ] Do you recall in detail the places you went and the routes you took on trips out of town?

L. [ ] Do you like to listen to music and have favorite singers and musicians?

BRAIN POWER DOUBLER #9 (cont'd)

M. [ ] Do you enjoy expressing yourself through drawing, sketching, or painting?

N. [ ] Do you like to spend time dancing?

O. [ ] Do you tend to organize things at home and at the office in patterns or by category?

P. [ ] Do you find it easy to interpret what other people do in terms of what they are feeling?

Q. [ ] Do you enjoy entertaining others with amusing or dramatic anecdotes?

R. [ ] Do you find boredom is sometimes relieved by hearing a variety of different sounds in your environment?

S. [ ] Do you see similarities or make connections between people you meet for the first time and people you already know?

T. [ ] Do you possess a strong sense of what you can and can't accomplish?

If you checked all three questions in any of the following groupings, rate that sense as one of your most strongly developed learning senses.

❑ The A, H, Q trio means you have strong linguistic senses.

❑ The F, L, R trio means you have strong musical senses.

❑ The C, G, O trio means you have strong logical and mathematical senses.

❑ The D, K, M trio means you have strong spatial senses.

❑ The E, I, N trio means you have strong kinesthetic senses.

❑ The J, P, T trio, you have strong intrapersonal senses.

❑ The B, J, S trio means you have strong interpersonal senses.

DISCOVERING YOUR BEST LEARNING RESOURCES

One person's meat is another person's poison applies equally to learning styles. What's learning sauce for the goose is not necessarily learning sauce for the gander.

Your boss may think she has done you a favor by sending you home with a videotape of the new steel fabricating system at work. But you might be the type who hates TV, rarely goes to movies, and prefers an evening at home curled up with a good magazine or book. In that case, you could find yourself chafing through the video, wishing you had a printed instruction manual so you could stop to reread sentences and sections and skim forward quickly at your own speed through passages that seem redundant.

How much faster do you think you would have learned if you could have read the same thing in printed form? How much more do you think you would have remembered the next day? How much less tired would it have made you, and how much easier would it have felt? How much do you feel your own personal learning power would have been multiplied?

Today there is an almost dangerous multiplicity of learning resources—the Internet, videos, CD-ROMs, books, magazines, brochures, workbooks, manuals, lecturers, seminars, hands-on workshops, courses, classes, demonstrations, and a whole lot more. You may think there are so many you could never keep track of them. But beneath its seeming complexity, knowledge can be conveyed in only five forms:

- ❑ The printed word—reports, memos, e-mail, newspapers, books, magazines, and so forth

- ❑ Personal experience—workshops, meetings, committees, simulations, conferences, and so forth

- ❑ The media—television, the Web, video- and audiotape, CD-ROM, film, slides, and so forth

- ❑ Exploring the world around you—documenting and encountering the subject firsthand, recording it, taking notes on what you see and hear, and so forth

- ❑ Other people—conversations, classes, seminars, lectures, and so forth

Figuring out which ones work best with your learning style can mean the difference between a positive learning outcome and a negative one. Match yourself with the wrong kind of resources for your PLS and you not only ensure a frustrating waste of time but another self-defeating learning experience that will only add to your own feeling that you weren't cut out to be a good learner. Select the right fit and you transform acquiring the information into an enjoyable, fast-paced opportunity (that leaves you feeling more confident than ever of your learning abilities).

Brain Power Doubler #10

Pretend you are considering becoming a nurse and wish to learn more about it. Use the following checklist to help match yourself with the kind of learning resources that work best for you. Place a checkmark by the statements that you feel apply most strongly to you.

If given my choice, I feel I learn best from

A. [ ] reading about it.

B. [ ] role playing through a typical experience under the guidance of a nurse.

C. [ ] listening to a lecture.

D. [ ] renting a videotape on the subject.

E. [ ] talking to experienced practical nurses.

F. [ ] visiting a school where private nurses are taught, videotaping one actually at work in the patient's home, and so forth.

G. [ ] posting a notice on the Web asking private nurses to e-mail accounts of their own experiences for you to read.

H. [ ] buying the audio book of a runaway bestselling account of her personal experiences by a private nurse and playing it in my car on the way to and from work.

I. [ ] working as an unpaid volunteer with private nurses for several months.

J. [ ] writing a report or speech based on any of the above experiences.

If any of the following duos applies to you, you probably are strong in that intelligence, even if you haven't cultivated it.

❏ If you checked A and G, one of your best learning resources is the printed word.

❏ If you checked B and I, one of your best learning resources is personal experience.

❏ If you checked D and H, one of your best learning resources is the media.

❏ If you checked F and J, one of your best learning resources is exploring the world around you.

❏ If you checked C and E, one of your best learning resources is other people.

MAXIMIZING YOUR PERSONAL LEARNING STYLE

Identifying your PLS and the best ways to use it can transform learning experiences. Let's say you have found you are a bottom-up learner who takes in information best visually and enjoys intrapersonal situations. Your boss suddenly asks you to bone up on the statistics on office-related accidents for a midweek meeting.

Before, you would have felt panicked and would have experienced difficulty locating the data, difficulty absorbing it, and difficulty in presenting it at the meeting. But now that you know your PLS, you can make a plan for gathering those statistics that draws entirely on your learning strengths.

As a bottom-up learner, you will want to focus on locating the specific states related to accidents in the office. Other facts and figures, how they are arrived at, and the history of statistics or accidents will not interest you and would only be a distraction. You want a textbook or an organized search at a library or on the World Wide Web, or if there were more time, you might seek out a class or lecture, any structured learning situation. The fact that your best learning senses are visual might send you to a lecture on a videocassette or off browsing Web sites. And since you learn well with and from others, you know a workshop or lecture, real or on tape, or talking one-on-one with somebody via the Web would be ideal.

Instead of feeling intimidated, you are now able to start off confidently with a plan that maximizes your learning strengths. Finding, absorbing, and remembering the most up-to-date figures on office-related accidents in time for your meeting will go faster. Your presentation will be clearer and more effective.

No matter what your own best learning styles or what you need to learn, the following step-by-step exercise will help you boost learning power by generating concrete ways of applying your PLS in any situations.

BRAIN POWER DOUBLER #11

Fill in the blanks in the following questionnaire. Let it be your guide to getting the most out of any learning opportunity.

1. I am a _____ learner.

2. When I have to begin learning about this particular subject, the best way for me to begin might be _____.

3. My two best learning senses are and _____ and _____. When learning about this, my most effective options for using these senses will be _____.

4. I learn best from these resources: _____. Matching resources available for learning about this are _____.

Chapter 4

MASTERING THREE STAGES OF LEARNING

Does this sound like a familiar situation? You studied hard for a review or test. You jumped up several mornings in a row. You pored over the material all day. You fell into bed weary at night. You were sure you had drummed it into your brain so thoroughly none of it could escape you.

Came the day of the test, you sat down, took pen in hand, and discovered to your horror that in spite of all your effort, the details had escaped you. You couldn't answer enough questions to pass the test, or at best you slid by among the bottom percentiles.

Where did you go wrong? You may have been studying hard, but you probably failed to make use of the entire learning process.

Acquiring the knowledge necessary to obtain a real estate license, for example, isn't just a matter of poring through the manuals. Learning researchers tell us it is an entire process. Just drilling yourself in a subject is to take advantage of only a tiny portion of the learning process.

According to scientists, this process develops through three stages:

❐ The period before learning

❐ The period (or periods) while we are learning

❐ The period after learning

Though you may not have realized it, the learning process begins the moment you become aware you need to learn something like a new software program or the cost of office chairs at five different stores. The process ends only when you have it down so pat you can never forget it or when there is no longer call for you to use the information.

69

Only a small amount of that time may be devoted to what you probably think of as "learning"—reading, studying, listening to experts. But the time before and after and even much of the time during acquiring knowledge offers overlooked opportunities for multiplying your learning power.

Before a new software program arrives, you could ask yourself what acquiring the information is likely to entail based on what you already know about software. If you don't know anything about software, you could ask a few friends who are familiar with it to give you pointers. While learning it, you could try to anticipate how various operations are likely to work, before you look them up or ask for help. Afterward, you could use the excitement of learning a new and challenging task to keep yourself thinking about the details until you know them by heart.

BEFORE LEARNING—PREPARATION, PLANNING, AND ACTION

Preparation is 90 percent of everything. Genius has been said to be 90 percent perspiration and 10 percent inspiration. The 90 percent law goes for learning too.

When two firms agree to merge, it may take only a few minutes to draw up and sign the letter of agreement. But arduous months—and perhaps years—of thought, study, and negotiation led up to that moment. Each firm investigated the other's assets, productivity, net worth, accounts payable, employee work load, future market, and a thousand other details before determining whether the merger should be consummated and under what terms.

When the Wright brothers flew at Kitty Hawk, it was the result of long, painstaking preparation. So was Madame Curie's discovery of the properties of radium. When Dawn Steel became the first woman to helm a major motion picture studio, years of work and planning lay behind her. When Windows 95 became the first software to debut with all the fanfare and first day sales usually reserved for a hit music album, that was the result of careful preparation too.

Sound preparation can pay 10 to 1 dividends in real life. Just a little preparation can double your reading power and help you get twice as much out of every second you spend absorbing something new.

Optimal learning studies have discovered that good learners—whether they realize it consciously or not—pave the way for their success with three essential steps. People who get the most out of their learning time

- ❑ Review what they already know about the subject.
- ❑ Target what they think will be the most important learning areas.
- ❑ Take whatever actions they can ahead of time for ensuring they learn what they intend to learn.

Brain Power Doubler #12

Next time—and every time—you have to learn anything, prepare beforehand. Try it once and you'll be converted for life.

1. Review everything you can draw from that might aid you in obtaining the most from the time you plan to spend learning. This includes the full extent of your current knowledge of the subject. But it also includes anything you know from other areas, however remote, that might be useful. (Insights into what you gained working at a local convenience store might be relevant to marketing. Experience with logical systems such as accounting might shed light while learning software.)

2. Based on what you have been told—or on what you want to know personally—list the 10 to 20 most important areas you believe are likely to be covered. You might couch this in the form of questions. Make your questions as specific as possible. (Is this software compatible with all the other programs I am using now? What are the basic differences in day-to-day use? What are the advantages? Where am I most likely to encounter trouble? Where do I call for help?)

3. Ask yourself if there is anything you can do beforehand to help you get more from the experience. (Might you read a book on the program designed to make it so simple even a small child could understand it? Or get someone with the same or similar program to let you practice on theirs?)

WHILE LEARNING "PROPOSITIONS" AND "REVISED PROPOSITIONS"

The key to the instant acquisition of knowledge is wholehearted mental and emotional involvement during the time you spend learning. When golfers want to learn a new golf swing, they pick it up quickly. When chefs want to learn a new cooking technique, they pick it up quickly.

They master new knowledge so fast because they love learning more about their passions. We all know people who are in love with what they do. They are so involved they eagerly seek to learn more every day. How can they fail to learn with attitudes like that?

You may feel, "Oh, that's easy to say. Those are exciting fields. I have to read through 50 pages of dry statistics on a company I doubt we will ever do business with and be able to report clearly on it to the senior vice president tomorrow. Try to get excited over that."

Granted, not everything you have to learn can be as exciting as French cuisine or improving your athletic ability. At first glance, a lot of stuff seems dull and boring by comparison. You might even think it could never be made interesting.

But Harvard Professor David Perkins has found a way to turn learning dross into gold. They're called "Propositions" and "Revised Propositions." These amazing mental superchargers will shift you from boredom to high gear no matter how dry and uninteresting the material to be learned appears.

Propositions are ideas and questions about why you are studying and what you expect to find out that you develop on the spot, as you are learning. It doesn't matter whether you are reading, listening to a lecture, or watching a video. If you want to get involved, and stay involved, ask questions and try to come up with ideas of your own about the subject from the moment you sit down to learn about something, throughout the experience, and until it's over.

At first, this advice might seem to run counter to your idea of how gaining knowledge works. You may believe that because the other person is an expert, you're supposed to be absorbing what he or she has to say. It seems to make sense that thinking intently to yourself the whole time would actually interfere with absorbing information.

But it's the opposite way around, according to Professor Perkins. Taking intelligent guesses in the form of Propositions and revising them in light of what you actually learn engages us intellectually and emotionally. You can think faster than you can read or than someone else can talk. That's one reason your mind gets restless and wanders, which is what really interferes with learning.

Propositions keep your attention from wandering. We feel excited when our projections are validated by what we read or hear next. We are less elated when we turn out wrong. Either way, the correct answer stands out and sticks in our heads.

BRAIN POWER DOUBLER #13

Throughout the remainder of this chapter and throughout all future learning situations, use Propositions and Revised Propositions to ensure you'll get more involved and come away with more at the end. You'll need a pad and pen (or a computer screen will do fine if the opportunity permits).

1. As soon as you have absorbed a sentence or two, start writing down your guesses about where things might be heading next. Keep doing this at intervals throughout. (Example: "A brief review of the old organization chart, then probably new job assignments." Or, "Likely to compare the situation among school teachers to the example being given of the woman who franchised her real estate firm just as the market became tremendously overvalued.)

2. Each time a new subject is introduced, try to guess how it will turn out. Write down what point you think will be made or what conclusion you believe will be reached. (Example: "News of declining enrollment in teacher's colleges—could imply less competition, better pay in future?)

3. Every time you are right make a large checkmark ($\sqrt{}$).

4. When you guess wrong, revise what you wrote to reflect the correct state of things. (Example: "Nope! Says will be three years before those classes graduate and reduced enrollment impacts the job market—till then the glut still means more teachers than jobs and reduced bargaining power with school boards.")

AFTER LEARNING—ATTACHING YOURSELF TO THE KNOWLEDGE

Most of us "let go" of a learning experience the minute it's over. We put away the article on practical nursing or leave the presentation on self-improvement, and that's the end of the learning experience for us. We often have so much else on our minds we hardly give what we heard or read another thought.

Research shows, however, that like the period before a learning experience, the period from a few hours to a few days afterward can be more decisive in determining what you get out of it than anything you do during it.

Were you ever an adolescent in love? Did you dwell for hours on the face and physique of your beloved after your encounters? Could you describe every detail without pausing to think?

Chances are you could. And the chances are the time you spent visualizing them afterward is the reason you could remember so well what your beloved looked like. It's true of important moments like an award for outstanding achievement, the day you open your own business, or the consummation of a big sale. You probably thought about them for days afterward and could remember who stood where and what the light was like coming through the window.

Get yourself that excited after you've reviewed a year's insurance statistics or listened to a presentation on global weather patterns and long-range economic forecasting and you'll be putting incalculable brain power to work on your behalf. That may sound like a tall order. But it's not.

You can take advantage of a well-established psychological technique to get yourself charged up afterward about complicated facts, figures, and the seemingly dullest or most irrelevant data. It's called "Attachment." It will have you as pleasurably preoccupied after learning next month's printing schedule as by something that could help you earn a raise or where your favorite singer's new record is on the charts.

Attachment operates on the principle that we spend the most time thinking about things that stir deep emotions in us. Whatever seems stupid, exciting, funny, threatening, or exceptionally positive returns to our mind again and again. Attachment is a seven-part strategy for getting your emotions stirred up over what you've learned, no matter how humdrum or tedious the content.

❏ Clear your mind of negative feelings about what you learned.

❏ Look for any possible way—unlikely or fanciful—you could benefit big time from what you learned.

❏ Identify the most interesting thing you learned.

❏ Try to recall anything funny.

❏ Try to remember anything that seemed stupid.

❏ Try to remember anything that made you mad.

❏ Try to remember anything that made you feel threatened.

BRAIN POWER DOUBLER #14

This is an essential part of all your learning. You are failing to make use of the full potential of your own brain power when you ignore it.

1. Clear your mind of any negative feelings about what you have learned. ("Insurance figures are boring." "Weather patterns have no long-term impact on the interior decoration business.")

2. Ask yourself if there is any possible way—however remote and fanciful—the information could be of big benefit to you. ("I'll have these figures down so pat at the meeting Thursday, my abilities will be recognized and I'll be promoted to regional manager." "This thing about the greenhouse effect turns out to be true. Since everyone will stay inside more, there will be increased emphasis on interior decorating.")

3. Ask yourself what the single most interesting thing was—however boring it might seem—and why it was interesting. ("That part about lost baggage claims from airports decreasing from 1 per 1,256.5 items handled to 1 every 1,788.3 items. Anything's an improvement. They lost one of my suitcases for a month. We can't forget that what all these statistics are about at bottom is people's lives.")

4. Ask yourself if anything struck you as funny. ("When I saw Sui Wong down in accounting make a face at the way the speaker droned through the part about this year's claims for damaged office furniture being a whole 3.5 percent higher." Or "When the speaker got mixed up and

BRAIN POWER DOUBLER #14 (cont'd)

said the weather below the equator in places like Egypt, Persia, and Mexico. Which are all way north.")

5. Ask yourself if anything struck you as particularly stupid or dumb. ("No one's ever going to be able to predict weather with near perfect accuracy weeks and even months ahead. Too much goes on up in the sky. Fronts stall. Clouds contain more moisture than expected. The jet stream suddenly bends up instead of down. They can't even predict stuff that big two days ahead.")

6. Ask yourself if there was anything that made you angry or mad. ("No one really needs to know whether gross claims are up 18.63 percent. It's the percentage of claims we pay that's important.")

7. Ask yourself if anything that was said made you feel threatened. ("Those who focused on electronic bulletin boards may well have wasted their efforts, considering the superiority of the Internet.")

DOUBLING YOUR
MEMORY POWER

Chapter 5

INSTANT MEMORY

Memory happens instantaneously. In a millisecond, as a matter of fact. When neurophysiologists Benjamin Libet and Bertram Feinstein of Mount Zion Hospital in San Francisco hooked people up to EEGs (machines that register brain waves), that's how long they found it took the mind to register perception. One thousandth of a second is all the time it takes for sight, sound, smell, emotion, thought—the elements that make up a memory—to travel down a nerve ending to your brain.

A second is short enough, about the time it takes to say millisecond. Trying to imagine it divided into half or even tenths is difficult. One thousandth of a second is inconceivable, a space so small the mind can't encompass it. Instantaneously, in other words.

Your memory of the words someone is saying or facts you're reading happens so fast it actually occurs before you can become consciously aware of them. Perceptions may reach your brain in a millisecond, Libet and Feinstein discovered, but it takes 999 thousandths of a second more for what you heard or read to be relayed to your conscious mind. Almost a whole second, in other words.

Memory may take place instantly. But this speed doesn't make memory ephemeral or faint. Once there, it lasts forever. In laboratory experiments, brain researcher Wilder Penfield stimulated the brain's memory banks and people recalled events—complete in every detail—from their past they thought they had forgotten. Everything you've ever felt, sensed, done, or experienced, Penfield concludes in *Mysteries of the Mind*, is still recorded somewhere within your brain.

Tragically and unnecessarily, research has also shown that we lose access to most of our memories within a brief span of time. Incredible as it seems, 50 percent of all we see and hear is gone within five minutes. Two thirds is lost before an hour is over. By the next day, the figure is 90 percent.

Yet it doesn't have to be that way. Your memories are still there, stored in your unconscious memory banks. It's really a matter of accessing them correctly, just as it is with retrieving files in a computer.

You can learn to get them back and to lock in key information instantly, so you can access it easier in the future. As you are about to discover, remembering is a skill, like math and relaxation, that can be learned. Before you have finished the next four chapters, you will have developed the knack of remembering more than 90 percent of everything you want to retain and recalling it at will. But even if you make use of only the four following techniques you'll find you have more than doubled your current memory power.

The strategies in this chapter strengthen your ability to remember by developing the mental circuits involved in memory. You may not realize it, but neuroscientists have discovered that mental exercise causes your brain to swell the same way exercise causes muscles to swell. When a broken finger is immobilized for a long time in a splint, the area of the brain that controls it shrinks. Conversely, when a finger is used in a new way or is exercised heavily the part of the brain that controls it grows.

FIVE STEPS TO INSTANT MEMORY

It's a well-known fact that many people can set their mental clock so that they can wake up precisely when they want to the next morning. Science has found the secret, and it's an ability anyone can learn.

You can use the same method to fix even the most complex data instantly into your memory. In essence, what you do is tag the information with a "mental charge." This charge lifts the information above other data and ensures your conscious mind will be able to locate it quickly and easily whenever you need to recall it.

"Instant Memory" is for when you find yourself faced without warning by important information that you know you will need to remember later. It's also amazingly easy to use. Just keep in mind these five simple words:

- ❏ Believe
- ❏ Intend
- ❏ Visualize
- ❏ Command
- ❏ Review

BRAIN POWER DOUBLER #15

If critical information comes at you unexpectedly and off the cuff while you're far away from a notebook or any other way to record it, don't panic. Follow these five foolproof steps:

1. Believe you will remember the material (this energizes the brain for remembering).

2. Intend to remember the material (putting genuine willpower into an effort doubles its chances for success).

3. Visualize or repeat the material once clearly in your mind.

4. Consciously tell yourself to remember the material.

5. Review your memory of the material the next day.

RECALL WHAT YOU MISSED WITH INSTANT REPLAY

How often have you berated yourself because you need to remember vital details from a critical conference or an important document and failed to take notes? Torture yourself no longer. It never has to happen again.

You can retrieve the information—all the salient details—with "Mental Review." Mental Review is a simple exercise that will help you recall any information—facts, names, nuances, your own insights— from events of the past few days in full detail and in "living color." It can also dramatically increase what you retain and understand of any critical information or experience.

Here's how Mental Review works:

- ☐ Describe in detail the situation in which you encountered the information.
- ☐ Set the scene.
- ☐ Use present tense.
- ☐ Try to recall the half-glimpsed details.
- ☐ Relate details to other details, facts, and ideas; look for new insights and connections.
- ☐ Continue till you recall everything important.
- ☐ Review and write down the information you wanted.

BRAIN POWER DOUBLER #16

Use this powerful review process anytime you missed significant details of a recent event.

1. Write down the entire experience or say aloud into a tape recorder. Don't just review things mentally. Speaking or writing them will help reinforce them and cause you to remember more details.

2. Set the scene—what you saw, heard, felt, touched, even your own feelings and reaction. Describe every detail. The more detail the better. You will find every detail you recall will stimulate a whole host of other details, each of which will trigger a whole flock of its own. (I am sitting in the conference room. The late afternoon sunlight is shining on the table. Carolyn is speaking. She is wearing a green sweater. . . .)

3. Stay in the present tense.

4. Devote three to five minutes to this portion of the exercise.

5. After you've described the scene, try to pull in the half-glimpsed details. (The speaker isn't wearing a wedding ring. . . .)

6. Relate these details to your other memories, looking for new insights. Look for as many connections as you can. (She talked about the success of their core line. But she said nothing about peripherals. Could there be a reason?)

7. Continue until you are sure you have recalled everything important.

8. Review your notes or replay the tape. Write down the information you were trying to remember.

CAPTURE COMPLEX DETAILS FOREVER WITH MENTAL REVIEW

Need to commit complex material to long-term memory? Try "Mental Review," a strategy developed by Professor Matthew Erdelyi of the City University of New York. It's highly effective for job procedures, client specs, company reports, business abstracts, lectures, speeches, board meetings, workshops, and any other situation in which you encounter detailed, complex material that you will have to call on for some time to come. Mental review empowers you to literally reverse the learning curve. Instead of forgetting 90 percent of complex information, you'll remember 90 percent. What's more, you'll be able to access it on demand for years.

❑ Ten minutes after learning, review for 5 minutes.

❑ After one day, review 2–3 minutes.

❑ After one week, review 2–3 minutes.

❑ After six months, review for 2–3 minutes.

Because you don't have to take written notes, many business people and executives use Mental Review to capture and reinforce key data that arise in impromptu conversations, during lunches, or at other social events.

BRAIN POWER DOUBLER #17

Use Mental Review the next time you need to capture the details in a long document or a spoken presentation.

1. Make a mental note of the points you want to remember. Maintain a running total of the number of points.

2. Ten minutes after the presentation is finished or you are through reading, find a place where you can be alone undisturbed for five minutes. Review the key points you wanted to remember.

3. Say each point out loud to yourself once. Don't repeat. It's not necessary.

4. If you find there are points you can't remember, don't push to recall them. Just make your best guess and go on.

> **BRAIN POWER DOUBLER #17** (cont'd)
>
> **5.** An hour later, have a review session. Repeat the preceding steps.
>
> **6.** Three hours afterward, repeat the process.
>
> **7.** Six hours later, do it once more.
>
> **8.** Right before going to sleep for the night, have a final review.
>
> **9.** Repeat the entire review process three times on days two and three.
>
> **10.** Keep the material fresh by having a review session every three to four days.

FORGET WHAT YOU DON'T NEED WITH MEMORY DELETE

One of the best ways to double your memory power is to double the amount of mental storage space available for new data and recollections. Our minds accumulate a lot of mental rubbish over the years, from obsolete names, dates, and numbers to once-important facts and figures we no longer need to know, to job procedures three jobs back, to directions on getting across town yesterday to a place you will never go to again.

You can free all that wasted mental space with your mind's Memory Delete function. With it you can erase what you no longer need to remember. Memory Delete is really Instant Memory in reverse.

Many software packages have a program that will delete unwanted files and programs. Your brain has one too. The next exercise will show you how to "boot up" your mind's Memory Delete program.

You have already acquired the basics when you learned Instant Memory. Now you put a variant of those five steps to work in reverse and use them to forget information instead of remembering it.

❏ Believe you will forget.

❏ Intend to forget.

❏ Visualize the information.

❏ Tell yourself to forget.

❏ Don't think about it again.

BRAIN POWER DOUBLER #18

At night, before you go to sleep, take a few minutes to banish obsolete data.

1. Pick something you want to forget, whether it's the kind of work you performed at your last job or a series of figures you memorized for last year's reports.

2. Believe you will forget it.

3. Intend to forget it.

4. Say out loud or visualize clearly what you want to forget.

5. Consciously tell yourself to forget it.

6. Don't think about it again. (If you do, don't dwell on the matter.)

Chapter 6

POWER MEMORY— USING MNEMONIC TECHNIQUES

Have you ever seen those memory wizards who walk through an audience of people they've never met before shaking hands and then remember all 100 or 200 names and match them with the right person? Did you envy their luck at being born with a such a fabulous memory?

If so, don't be fooled. Your envy was misplaced. As with so many other things, memory wizards aren't born—they're made. The ability to remember every name you hear, every fact you study, every concept you learn isn't an inherited trait. It's a mental trick anyone can learn.

Developing a phenomenal memory isn't hard work. It uses your brain's natural capacities—capacities that usually go untapped. The technique is so basic it has been successfully taught to children.

No matter how bad you think your memory is, this technique is guaranteed to make you the equal of any so-called memory wizard. Professionals call it "mnemonics." That dresses it up and makes it sound scientific. Calling it mnemonics also makes it seem difficult and technical. That scares many people and puts them off when they first hear the term.

Actually, mnemonics are nothing more than the ability of the mind to associate words, ideas, and images. Think of it as "association" rather than "mnemonics" and you'll find it sounds far less intimidating and far more natural.

It has long been known that information becomes locked permanently in the mind when it is associated with something vivid, interesting, or unusual. This led to the old school of spanking or otherwise punishing children to reinforce rules that were not to be broken. Association is also the way most of us learned how to spell the title of the person who ran our grade school—we simply envisioned her with her arm around our shoulders being a "pal" as in "principal."

Association is a means of "tagging" or "labeling"—computer folk would call it "addressing"—information you may need for future reference. People use it to keep track of material relating to hobbies, their professions, even facts about people and places that interest them. A stockbroker uses it to remain abreast of important data in the realms of business publications he reviews each week. An entertainment executive uses association to keep track of the names of all the people, records, songs, movies, and television shows she hears of and impresses the artists and actors responsible later by seeming to know all about their careers. Because of it, an amateur chef is able to recall in detail any one of thousands of recipes he has read over the years and reproduce it exquisitely for dinner guests. A corporate attorney who must cope with constantly changing governmental rules and regulations uses association to pinpoint rules that apply to new and ongoing work.

This chapter will focus on four powerful associative or mnemonic techniques, each a classic method for multiplying memory power that will rarely, if ever, fail. Each technique shares a common factor, associating information around easy-to-remember elements and outrageous, unforgettable images. But each also draws on different mental abilities—visual, verbal, mathematical, logical—and yields the best results for different individuals. These four associative strategies are

❑ The Loci Technique
❑ Pegwords
❑ Acronyms
❑ Data indexing

LOCATING MEMORY WITH THE LOCI TECHNIQUE

Want a fail-safe memory doubler? Here's one that has stood the test of time for more than 2,500 years! Roman orators used it to organize their speeches; memory wizards rest their success on its capable shoulders; salesmen have used it to keep track of customer names; and students have squeezed by exams on the strength of it alone.

It's the Loci Technique. Like the memory techniques that follow, it harnesses your mind's ability to associate one idea or image with another. At some point in your childhood, you probably were subjected to some variant of the old joke, "Don't think of a blue cow." Likely you found it hard not to think of that color cow once the image was implanted.

The Loci Technique makes use of this psychological trick to associate stuff you'll need to recall with mental images of places you know. (The name derives from the Latin word for place, *locus*—plural is *loci*.) The more bizarre or dramatic you make the image and combination the more vividly you'll be able to mentally locate the associated information later.

All you need to do is pick a specific set of places that you will use over and over to help fix important names and data in your memory, for example, these five common areas found in most living rooms: (1) the main doorway, (2) your sofa, (3) the television set, (4) your lamp, (5) a picture on the wall.

It's a simple process:

❒ Select the facts, figures, or other data to be remembered.

❒ Pick elements that relate to the five loci or places in your living room—doorway, your sofa, TV, lamp, picture on the wall.

❒ Create visual images that incorporate the information with items from your living room.

❒ Run these images through your head several times a day for three or four days.

For instance, the name of a new client named Ms. Ashland. She is tall. Envision her standing in your doorway, her head hitting the jam. Envision a forest fire turning everything to ash on the television. Envision the picture on your wall containing a beautiful landscape.

When you meet her again, don't worry about going blank on her name. Think about your living room. That will suggest the image of her coming in the doorway and hitting her head. Then think of what was on your television at the time; that will stimulate the picture of the forest fire turning everything to ash. Remember what the picture looked like—a landscape.

Bang! The name "Ashland" will be on the tip of your tongue.

BRAIN POWER DOUBLER #19

If you are visually oriented, use the Loci Technique to create vivid mental images that will lock names, dates, facts, and figures in your memory.

1. Select the items you want to remember. (The figure 207, for instance.)

2. Relate it to one or more of the five loci or places in your living room—doorway, sofa, TV, lamp, picture. (Let's make it the picture and the television.)

3. Create visual images that incorporate data with the items from your living room. (Visualize the painting being a hideous green face with a price tag of $207 hanging off it—that you are kicking yourself mentally for purchasing. Visualize the television under the painting with a repairman fixing it; he presents a $207 bill at the end.)

4. Review these images in your head several times a day for three or four days.

5. Next week try to recall the figure associated with them. (Bring the picture to mind, the hideous green face—what price was it? Ditto for the television repair bill. You will be surprised at how easy they are to recall.)

PINNING DOWN MEMORY WITH PEGWORDS

"Mary had a little lamb. Its fleece was white as snow. And everywhere that Mary went, that lamb was sure to go." Or "This old man, he played one; he played knick-knack on my thumb." No one ever forgets these snippets of childhood rhyme.

Our most remote ancestors were already aware of the power of rhyme to help pin down memory. Stories and legends of heroes, heroines, and gods were put in rhyme. Rhyme made things easier to remember because the end of one line gave a cue to the sound of the word that ended the next line and therefore to what preceded that word.

Most of us remember hundreds—even thousands—of couplets, snatches of poetry, and entire songs because of the power of rhyme to snare mind and memory. "Double, double, toil and trouble. Fire burn and cauldron bubble," we hear Shakespeare's witches whisper once—and remember it always. And when we hear the phrase, "Roses are red, violets are blue," we know that the concluding word of the phrase that follows will be "you."

What memory experts call Pegwords works in a similar fashion. It combines a contemporary scientific approach with the ancient power of rhyme. The result is an infallible memory system that many people consider second to none.

Pegwords link mental images for critical facts and figures with specific rhymes to the numbers one through ten—"one" and "sun," for instance, or "six" and "sticks." The rhymes are your Pegwords.

Pegwords work especially well for those with mathematical or verbal orientations, but anyone can use them with remarkable results. As with the Loci System, you start by choosing a series of objects.

You can make up your own rhyming system if you want. But in his book *Mastering the Information Age*, Michael McCarthy offers the following ready-made pairings:

One - sun	Six - sticks
Two - shoe	Seven - heaven
Three - tree	Eight - gate
Four - door	Nine - vine
Five - hive	Ten - hen

Here's how Pegwords help you boost memory power when you have vital information you need to remember:

❑ Pinpoint as specifically as possible the facts, names, or ideas you want to remember.

❑ Create a mental image that links that information to the objects. (Pegwords such as "sun" and "sticks") that rhyme with the numbers.

❑ When you need to recall the data, mentally review the numbers, and the image associated with the rhyming Pegword will pop right up, bringing the information you want with it.

Learning whiz Michael McCarthy offers this example: "Suppose you want to recall several points to bring up in a staff meeting: expanding the telephone system, finishing projects in a more timely manner, and allocating tasks for a specific project. For the first point (one-sun-telephone), imagine a giant telephone floating in the sky with rays of the sun radiating out from it. For the second point (two-shoe-timely completion), see yourself at your desk stamping stacks of paper "Completed" with a giant shoe. For extra inputting strength, hear the "thud" of the shoe as it hits the pile of papers. For the third point (three-tree-allocation), visualize the people in the office sitting on branches of a tree, working away at various aspects of the project."

Take a minute to fix these images and rhymes in your mind. Tomorrow, try to recall the facts they represent using these Pegwords. You'll be impressed with how easy they are to remember.

Brain Power Doubler #20

This exercise shows you how to apply Pegwords to crucial material you can't chance forgetting.

1. Pinpoint as specifically as possible the facts, names, or ideas you want to remember.

2. Create a mental image that links that information to the objects (Pegwords such as "sun" and sticks") that rhyme with the numbers.

3. When you need to recall the data, mentally review the numbers and the image associated with the rhyming Pegword will pop right up bringing the information you want with it.

ASSOCIATING MEMORY WITH ACRONYMS

How do you remember "E-G-B-D-F"—the order of the letters representing the musical notes on the musical staff? Is it by repeating the phrase "every good boy does fine" to yourself? It is for most people.

What about the Great Lakes? In many geography classes, teachers locked them into students' memories forever with a single word. Does that sound like magic? It is! Verbal magic. That one word was "homes." It's made up of the first letter of the names of each of the five lakes. That's *H* for Huron, *O* for Ontario, *M* for Michigan, *E* for Erie, and *S* for Superior.

"Homes," like "every good boy . . . ," is an acronym. You've seen them all your life—and many times during the typical day. Acronyms have grown from a memory trick to a staple of the modern world, necessary to help us remember the proliferations of companies, government agencies, and charities that surround us on all sides.

Acronyms are words or sentences designed to enhance memory power by reminding you of the first letters of important items you will need to recall later. "MADD"—for the organization Mothers Against Drunk Driving is famous. How many more can you recall offhand? Likely it's a large number, attesting to the efficacy of acronyms.

If you drive often, you will doubtless have noticed that many "personalized" license plates contain acronyms. Recently, I've seen LTRYWNR for "lottery winner"; HZNHRZ for "his and hers"; and WGESLV for "wage slave."

If you do well at Scrabble, crossword puzzles, and other word games, acronyms are a natural way for you to lock information in your memory. Even if you aren't some sort of linguistic whiz, you'll find creating acronyms is not very hard, once you get the knack. The effect of acronyms on our memory is so potent you can even use them to recall unrelated words and dates.

- ❐ List the first letters of the name or word for each item you wish to remember.

- ❐ Rearrange and transpose letters until they form a word or the first letters of the words in a sentence.

- ❐ Be creative.

- ❐ If you're short on vowels or consonants, fill in (you'll discover they are no barrier to remembering the key letters in your acronym).

Take the four mnemonic techniques presented in this chapter. Can you remember the names of all three? Would you be able to remember them tomorrow? Why not try to make an acronym of their first letters? They consist of *L* for the Loci Technique, *P* for Pegwords, *A* for Acronyms, and *D* for Data Indexing. That's *L, P, A, D*.

This might not at first look like a promising set of letters to work with. It's mostly consonants, only a single vowel. But remember, be creative—you can fill in the vowels if you need them. Try rearranging the letters a bit. Transpose the first letter to the end, for instance. The result is P-A-D-L. That sounds like "paddle" and you could remember it with this name. Reinforce it with an image of someone who forgot the four mnemonic techniques being "paddled."

Tomorrow ask yourself what the four mnemonic techniques are. The odds are high you will recall the letters P-A-D-L and immediately associate the Loci Technique, Pegwords, Acronyms, and Data Indexing with them.

Or make up a sentence with the first letter of each word the first letter of each one of the techniques: *L, P, A, D*. For something lively enough to stick in your imagination, you could come up with, "Lively Pandas Always Dance." Envision a lively panda dancing and you'll find you can remember the Loci Technique, Pegwords, Acronyms, and Data Indexing months and even years from now.

BRAIN POWER DOUBLER #21

Use acronyms whenever there's a list of items you will need to recall. Take your time with each of the four steps and you'll have the life-saving, memory-saving ability of acronyms at your service.

1. Make a list of the items you will want to recall later. (For example, let's go back to the Loci Technique, Pegwords, Acronyms, and Data Indexing.)

2. Jot down the first letter of each item. (Say, *L, P, A, D*.)

3. Write them down in different orders and try pronouncing the result. (In addition to "P-A-D-L," you can get "L-A-P-D." That pronounces something like "lapped.")

4. When you find one that sounds like a real word, create an image that makes it easier for you to remember that word. (Can you think of an image to associate memory and lapped?)

DESIGNATING MEMORY WITH DATA INDEXING

Have you ever looked at a room full of filing cabinets or read the label on a "1-gigabyte" hard drive enviously. Did you wish you could consciously store everything you need to remember, index it as accurately, and retrieve it as quickly?

Don't despair. Data Indexing gives you the brain power to do that. You can create your own infinitely expandable mental card file, filing cabinet, or data storage program.

According to scientists, our brains are capable of retaining about 100 billion bits of information. That's the equivalent of 500 encyclopedias! The difficulty is locating and retrieving the specific bit of data you need instantly and easily when you need it.

Mostly that information sits there the same way you acquired it, random and jumbled. Searching your mind in vain for it is a frustrating experience and often doomed to failure. It's like walking into a vast warehouse many city blocks wide holding an important letter and having to search for it one room at a time.

But what if you had a map of the warehouse, an index to the 500 encyclopedias' worth of memories and data stored in your brain? You'd multiply your brain power by 500 times when it comes to memory.

With Data Indexing, you'll discover how to create a virtually infallible mental reference guide to those 100 billion bits of information. Brain power expert Scott Witt compares the power of Data Indexing to 33 pages of information. One page of index in the average book, Witt points out, summarizes the key ideas in 33 pages of text. "Which would be easier to do," he asks, "memorize one index page or the 33 pages of text it covers?"

Data Indexing works in much the same way as do the labels on files or the "address" on computer data. You mentally assign a tag or label to the information that makes it difficult to forget. When you index—and subreference and subsubreference—you can consciously store and access an almost infinite amount of data.

Data Indexing is easy. It works memory miracles for everyone, but those who are logically oriented will find it particularly suited to their abilities. Data Indexing involves only four mental steps:

❏ Source Identifier—a "tag" that tells where the data to be indexed came from

❏ Subject Label—a "tag" that tells what category the data is being indexed under

❏ Data Linking—associating the facts to both subject and source

❏ Index subordinate data through the same process

In *How to Be Twice as Smart,* Witt offers the example of someone wanting to index information from his book *Spare-Time Businesses You Can Start and Run for Less than $1,500.* He suggests using "$1,500" as the Source Identifier, since it is unique to the book. Then create a mental picture of your mail-order business selling items that are price-tagged $1,500 each. Since one section is on mail order advertising and another is dedicated to catalogues, he suggests using these as Subject Labels. Finally he recommends creating an unforgettable address by linking the subject and source with a memorable mental image.

The great advantage of Data Indexing is that you never consciously memorize anything. You don't have to. Just hooking the images and labels together this way creates a mental filing system as good as any secretary or computer programmer ever created.

BRAIN POWER DOUBLER #22

Use Data Indexing for mentally filing names, dates, figures, facts, concepts, and any other kind of information you believe may prove critical in the future.

1. Create a mental Source Identifier that will help you recall where the data came from. (Material from Professor Lincoln's Brainstorming Seminar, for instance, could be tagged, "Prof. Lincoln's Seminar.")

2. Create a Subject Label to file the data under. (For instance, say the main topic was "Brainstorming"—you could use that word as your subject tag. In fact, associate all future information about brainstorming with it.)

3. Create a Data Linking image between them. (Envision the professor dressed as Lincoln, stovepipe hat, beard, standing at the front of the class, a cloud pouring rain down on his head—a "brain storm.")

4. Link subordinate ideas. (A description of the six modes of thinking could be linked by an image of the professor with six storms circling his head—try to forget that image, if you can.)

Chapter 7

MEMORY MAPS—
THE POWER OF PERSONALIZING

You're about to become acquainted with a powerful new tool for locking information in your memory. Called Memory Maps (or mind maps), learning experts have been developing it over the last decade or so. The technique is so simple it seems almost like a kid's game. All you do is jot down key ideas and facts and draw arrows to indicate connections or associations between them.

But Memory Mapping is much more than child's play. CEOs of multinational corporations, software developers, entrepreneurs, college professors, and students are all using it to boost memory power and stimulate thinking. It's great for meetings and lectures and for any time you have an opportunity to jot notes. When you catch information "on the fly" or can't use Memory Map when it's first presented, use Memory Mapping later to crystallize the information and store it in your mental hard drive.

Memory Mapping is derived from the work of Canadian psychologist Endel Tulving. He gave two groups of students 100 cards with words printed on one side. He asked one group to memorize the words. He asked the other to organize them into what seemed logical categories to them.

Afterward Tulving tested both groups to see how many of the 100 words they remembered. Surprisingly, those who had merely organized the words without making any special effort to remember them scored just as well on the test as students who concentrated on memorizing them. Tulving concluded that the students' active involvement in organizing the material provided meaningful patterns and associations that reinforce data in our memory as effectively as conscious effort to remember it.

Memory Mapping involves writing a key word from something you want to remember in the center of a sheet of paper. Important subideas are written nearby, and lines are drawn between them and the central idea. Ideas that connect to the subideas are then jotted down, and a line is drawn to connect them. Some of these may connect to the main idea, or they may not. The final result looks like a doodle or a kid's drawing, with dozens of branching clusters.

It is more fun to store information this way than through linear note taking, and it's easier to locate key ideas later at a glance. It's great for classes, sales meetings, books, reports, videos, television documentaries, audio tapes, anywhere that information is being disseminated verbally or visually.

Memory Mapping works because in the process of writing down key concepts and drawing the connections you think about, understand, and evaluate the information while translating it into terms you personally can relate to. It's particularly useful for those with high visual (as opposed to verbal) intelligence, who feel stifled by the need to outline in a linear form. But it is simple and powerful enough to be used effectively by anyone.

Pictured is a typical Memory Map.

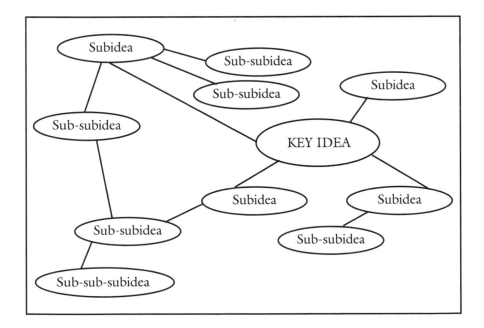

This Memory Map might be confusing, just a mishmash of labels and lines. But begin in the center with the Key Idea and things will soon start to make sense. Follow the lines that move away from there; they terminate in secondary or subideas. Lines radiate from these subideas to subordinate ideas or sub-subideas. Other lines show connections between these subideas and sub-subideas and the Key Idea or with each other.

Memory Mapping is a powerful memory enhancer because it works on a number of levels at once.

❒ Diagramming information converts the incoming mass of data into concepts and images that are meaningful to you.

❒ It draws on the left-brain verbal, analytical abilities *and* the right-brain spatial, visual abilities, reinforcing facts and data simultaneously in the memory circuits on both sides of your brain.

❒ By jotting down key ideas and indicating connections between them, you personalize the data, arranging them in a way that is meaningful to you.

❒ Because there is always space for further ideas and connections, you are prodded to keep looking in new directions.

❒ Since the key elements are all right there on one sheet it's easier for you to see important connections.

❒ Information is organized around your own perception of how the ideas are associated, making them more likely to lodge in your memory and easier to recall.

❒ Consciously processing the information—rather than passively listening or reading—makes it more likely you will remember it.

❒ Connecting ideas in a nonlinear fashion is actually a powerful memory enhancer, working with the natural grain of the mind, which links memories the same way.

MEMORY MAPPING MADE EASY

Stop for a moment. Think back over your life to moments when you suddenly mastered a difficult task or figured out something hard to understand. They stick in your memory, don't they? You still remember the skill acquired or the facts you learned.

That's the power of personal involvement. That's also why Memory Maps make such powerful tools for reinforcing facts and figures while you learn or later. Identifying what you feel is important, jotting down key words, drawing connections, pinpointing relationships all generate personal involvement. This doubles memory power by ensuring you'll remember what you map better and longer and more easily than you will by passive listening, reading, or taking notes.

Memory Mapping is easy, too. All you need is a large sheet of paper and a pencil. The larger the sheet of paper, the better—one of those large-size art or chart-size pads is best. But millions of Memory Maps have been drawn on standard 8-1/2 × 11 sheets of paper. By all means, use a pen if that's all you've got. You may however, want to alter elements as you find better words or discover a connection you want to change, and it's easier to erase with a pencil.

One writer I met even uses colored pencils. He recommended having three to five separate colors to help distinguish different kinds of connections and types of ideas. He uses one color of pencil to distinguish what he actually learned new, another for things from his own experience, and a third for information he needed to follow up and research later. Still others were reserved for subideas and sub-subideas.

Memory Mapping involves six strategic steps:

❑ Write a key idea or fact you want to remember in the center of the page and draw a circle around it.

❑ Nearby, jot down any important related ideas or subideas that occur to you and remember to circle each.

❑ Draw lines connecting these ideas to your central idea.

❑ Jot down specific examples, references, or thoughts implied by your subideas and connect them.

❑ Keep adding ideas and connections as they occur to you until you feel you have captured everything important.

❑ Continue to make additions later if anything important suggests itself.

Here are some tips drawn from leading proponents of Memory Mapping that will help you get the most from your efforts. Don't worry about whether an idea is important enough or not. You can always erase it, move it, or change it by inserting a new, more important item in its circle. To give yourself even more options for changing your mind, leave room for new circles that may occur to you later. Your map doesn't have to be complete or "academically" accurate. It's your personal record, and as long as it suits your needs, that's all that matters. The only purpose of a Memory Map is to create and capture thoughts and data you consider vital, in your own way.

For shorthand, you can use any visual symbols that have meaning for you—dollar signs, cartoons, whatever. Place a dollar sign next to elements that relate to increasing your own income. Put an *X* or a skull and crossbones by things you have been warned to avoid. Or try a question mark by figures you need to double-check.

The next exercise is designed to introduce you to Memory Mapping as simply as possible. It will give you immediate experience putting your knowledge of Memory Mapping to work.

Brain Power Doubler #23

Make a Memory Map of what you consider the key ideas in this chapter. Get a pencil and that large sheet of paper mentioned earlier. (A partial Memory Map of this chapter follows to help get you started. Simply fill in the rest.)

1. Put a word or two representing what you consider the main subject of the chapter in the center of the page and circle it.

2. Next pencil in the two or three key subideas and draw lines connecting them to the central idea.

3. Examine each subidea one at a time and add any ideas they suggested in a cluster around them.

4. Then examine each sub-subidea and jot down any subsidiary ideas they might suggest and so on until you feel you have included everything important.

5. Leave room for new circles to contain any ideas or relevant facts that you learn or think of later.

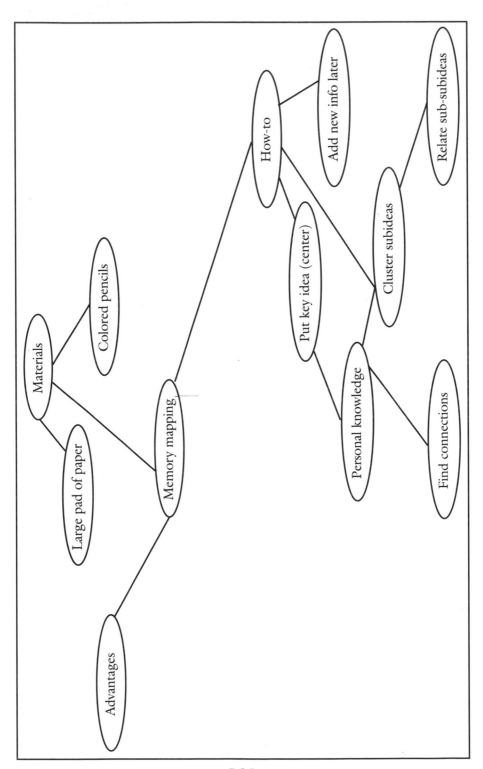

MASTERING THE ESSENTIALS OF MEMORY MAPPING

How effective is Memory Mapping at increasing memory power? Ask Jan DeGroot. "It's just doodling," Jan scoffed the first time he heard about it. Jan headed a Boston financial institution with branches throughout the state that was about to swell its size through merger with a rival organization.

I suggested a simple stratagem for putting the power of Memory Mapping to the test. It's one you can try too. I told Jan to have his assistant take notes the old-fashioned way during the next merger meeting, while he used Memory Mapping to keep track of important details. (You can make the same arrangement with a friend for a lecture or meeting.) At the end of the day, they were to each sit down and, without reference to their earlier notes, try to write down as many key items as they could remember. The results astonished both Jan and his assistant. Jan's list contained almost double the number of details. You'll be astonished at the results too if you give Memory Mapping a try.

Memory Mapping is a lifesaver in almost any learning experience. Say you were caught flat-footed in the hall at the office and were given rapid fire data you weren't in a position to write down. Say events prevented you from scribbling them down as notes afterward. Even days later, the power of Memory Mapping to summon associated memories from the unconscious is so strong that if you began to map what you heard in the hall, you would generate nearly 100 percent recall.

BRAIN POWER DOUBLER #24

You can use the following exercise to map key information you want to remember no matter what form it comes in, visual, verbal, or print. You can use it right then or days, weeks, and even months later.

1. Get a sheet of paper and a pencil.
2. Write the key fact—or a key fact (it doesn't matter)—in the center of the page.
3. Circle it and all subsequent items you write down.
4. Write important related ideas or subideas around it in a cluster.
5. Draw lines connecting these subideas to the central circle.
6. Note any relationships between subideas with a connecting line.
7. Cluster any ideas related to your subideas around them and draw the appropriate connections. Note any relationships between these sub-subideas and other subideas or your central idea.
8. Continue until finished.

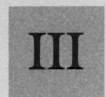

III

DOUBLING YOUR
READING POWER

INSTANT READING

Procedures, e-mail, reports, memoranda, Web sites, letters, newspapers, faxes, journals—in whatever form, an enormous portion of what we are called upon to learn and remember every day comes to us via the written word. Before computers, everyone used to complain that they didn't have enough time to keep up with their reading (for example, the quotient of newspapers, magazine articles, and books necessary to feel adequately informed).

With the advent of the home and office PC, things have gotten only worse, not better. Reports, brochures, memos, magazines, and books are still there. But to them has been added fax/modems, e-mail, the Internet, and the World Wide Web, and we are challenged to encompass it all if we are to succeed at our jobs, make informed choices, and lead more fulfilling lives. We are now called upon to read and absorb more material conveyed through print than any generation in history. Today, even speed readers report feeling overwhelmed. It's easy to see why a boost in your reading power means a boost in your brain power. But don't let yourself be intimidated. New reading strategies allow you to turn the situation around, lift all that information off your shoulders, and put it to work for you—turn it from an obstacle to an asset.

Science has learned a lot about reading in the last 30 years. Powerful as it is, speed reading was only the beginning. Most people think speed reading is pretty exciting and at the cutting edge. And it's a great advance over the way most of us were taught to read. But speed reading *was* only a beginning. New reading strategies make speed reading obsolete. They unleash natural reading abilities so powerful you can read anything almost instantly, without sacrificing comprehension or understanding. And unlike speed reading, they work without your having to master complex exercises and skills.

What if, by the time you woke up tomorrow morning, you could double your own reading power? What if you could glide through reports, newspaper articles, e-mail, Web sites, spreadsheets, and books without working up a sweat? What if you could read virtually anything and everything, instantly?

Finish this chapter before you go to sleep tonight and apply its principles; you'll have just that ability when you wake up. You're about to encounter instant reading strategies that will double your reading speed and increase comprehension.

If that sounds like overclaiming, it's not. Your natural reading abilities, like all your other mental abilities, are literally that powerful. University research has shown that just one of the following Reading Doublers, backtracking, increases your reading speed by 100 percent.

CONCENTRATION: THE KEY TO INSTANT READING

What? You may be saying. Something as simple as concentrating harder gives me an ability like Instant Reading? Ridiculous! It may sound too good to be true. But it's backed up by sound scientific evidence. Merely focusing more intently on what you read catapults your speed and comprehension light years ahead.

Just consider the following. Have you ever been in an intense situation—one involving danger perhaps, such as a car suddenly bearing straight for you, or seeing someone in peril—in which you looked up and took in every detail of the scene at a glance? If so, then you know the brain's amazing capacity to instantly and comprehensively perceive whatever the eye takes in.

Or think about the times you've plowed through paragraphs or even whole pages of a work-related document, only to come to the sudden realization that you have no idea of what you have been reading. Think about how much reading time you lose just through lack of concentration, through failing to read with conscious intent.

In his landmark work, *How to Read Better and Faster,* reading instructor Norman Lewis chronicled the powerful connection between concentration and reading speed. During an experiment at his Adult Reading Laboratory, Lewis had volunteers read a short article at their normal speed. He provided comfortable surroundings and an atmosphere conducive to relaxation. The volunteers were asked to read material at the same pace they typically did at home. The only stipulation was that they read every word and strive for comprehension. Afterward, Lewis recorded their reading times and tested them for comprehension.

The next day, Lewis had his volunteers read a second article of the same length. This time, he asked them to read through it as fast as they could. Again, the one stipulation was that they were to read every word and not sacrifice comprehension. Again, Lewis recorded participants' speeds and tested them for comprehension afterward.

The results provided dramatic evidence of the power of concentration. Most volunteers had read 25 percent to 50 percent faster, and their comprehension was undiminished.

Brain Power Doubler #25

You'll soon be reading near your full speed—instead of poking along at your present rate.

1. Determine your optimum reading speed. Find something you can read at one sitting, preferably a newspaper article or a chapter of a book.

2. Make a mark halfway through the piece you plan to read.

3. Note the time and begin reading.

4. When you reach the halfway mark, stop reading for a moment and note how long it has taken you to read the first half of the piece.

5. Continue reading—only this time concentrate on pressing yourself to read faster. But don't read so fast you sacrifice comprehension.

6. When you reach the end, take note of the time again. Notice how much more quickly you were able to read the second half when you consciously concentrated on increasing your speed. Imagine saving that much time—every time you read. Then imagine saving twice as much time, by just concentrating on reading a little bit faster still.

7. The next time you read—and every time you read—consciously concentrate on reading just a bit faster—the results over even a few days or a week will amaze you.

OVERCOMING THE THREE BAD HABITS OF READING

Before you can learn to read faster, you need to overcome three counterproductive habits we all learned in elementary school. Unless taught
otherwise since then, we unwittingly repeat them over and over count-
less hundreds of times throughout each reading session. This multiplies
the work many times over. No wonder we plod so slowly and reading
makes us tired so soon.

The three bad habits of reading are

❏ Subvocalization.

❏ Word-for-word reading.

❏ Regression.

You may never have heard of them before. You may not have been
aware you had them. But once you learn about them, chances are you'll
realize they have been inhibiting your reading speed all your life.

These three habits are like millstones. With them around your
neck, instant reading is impossible. Drop any one of them and you will
leap far ahead in reading power. Overcome all three and you will find
you have already developed into something of an instant reader in the
process.

Subvocalization: Repeating the Words as You Read Them

Likely you learned to read by following along with the teacher and
repeating the letters, then words, then sentences under your breath as
she read them. This is what scientists call "subvocalizaton."

Repeating words under your breath as you read slows you down
to the speed of the spoken word. Your brain can think words—and read
words—a whole lot faster than you can talk. That's why your tongue
gets twisted sometimes, when it can't keep up with your brain.

And no wonder. The fastest you can read when you sound out
each word mentally, according to reading expert Michael McCarthy,
author of *Mastering the Information Age,* is about 150 words per
minute. The top speed for people who read word by word is 200 to
300 words per minute. That's almost half the 600-plus words per
minute the average person reads.

Overcoming subvocalization can be tricky at first. It's a lot like learning to ride a two-wheel bicycle for the first time. You may fall off a few times at the beginning. But stick with it a while and you'll acquire the knack. And as with riding a bike, once you learn the knack, you never lose it again.

BRAIN POWER DOUBLER #26

The following exercise is basic to all forms of instant reading. It will help you determine whether you subvocalize and help you stop doing it. Don't skip it. That's because subvocalization is the number-one stumbling block to faster reading.

1. Ask yourself if you subvocalize while you read.

2. You may not be able to answer. How you read may be such second nature to you that you've never thought about it consciously. If so, pay attention to whether you repeat the words to yourself as you read.

3. If you find you are a subvocalizer, and it's likely you are, try to read the rest of this chapter a little faster than you can repeat words. Press yourself and attempt to let your eye take in the words without pausing to say them to yourself. You may even find yourself going faster than you think you can take in information from the printed page. That's okay, too.

4. When you reach the end of this chapter, stop. Write down what you remember as the key points.

5. Return to this spot. Now review the chapter. You'll be astonished at how much you did retain.

6. Continue to practice this technique until you no longer find yourself subvocalizing from habit.

From Word-at-a-Time Reading to Phrase-at-a-Time Reading

Originally, we learned to read one word at a time. We discovered the sound and meaning of each word, as our teachers taught it to us. Then we learned to associate individual words together one at a time in strings. "See . . . Spot . . . run." It's a terrific system for learning to read. But it's a bad system for actually reading.

One reason you may not like reading is that it slows you down. You can think—and live—a whole lot faster than you can read. Reading feels like plodding slowly toward an unreachable and not very important goal.

Surveys show that people who can leave word-by-word reading behind can easily learn to read at 600, 1,000, and even 2,000 words per minute. That's many times the speed of someone who still chugs along mentally reciting each word to him or herself one at a time.

Research has yielded a whole new and far more efficient way for adults to read. By the time we are out of childhood, our minds are able to grasp larger chunks of material. We take advantage of that ability and make a quantum jump beyond our old-fashioned word-by-word efforts.

If you're a word-at-a-time reader, the thought of a whole new way of reading may seem far-fetched. But it's soundly based. Certainly you'll grant that your adult brain can take in and understand larger chunks of data than you could as an elementary schooler. You might not have connected the two. But your ability to pick up and manage larger chunks of information applies to reading as well.

The adult brain is hardwired to pick up and interpret whole phrases at a glance, without your having to decode or sound them out word by word. Rather than limping along word by word, you can learn to read phrase by phrase. If each phrase consists of only three words, you will be tripling your reading speed.

Most information is contained in short phrases (each of which expresses a whole idea) within sentences anyway. Just look for small groups of connected words such as "Most information" . . . "is contained" . . . "in short phrases" . . . "within sentences anyway."

Take the sentence that ends the paragraph before the last: "If each phrase consists of only three words, you will be tripling your reading speed." If you read it word for word, you saw it as individual elements something like this: "If . . . each . . . phrase . . . consists . . . of . . . only . . . three . . . words, . . . you . . . will . . . be . . . tripling . . . your . . . reading . . . speed."

But what if your eye were trained to make use of the brain's capacity for perceiving printed matter phrase by phrase? You would see the same sentence something like this: "If each phrase . . . consists of . . . only three words . . . you will be . . . tripling . . . your reading speed. Phrase-by-phrase reading will liberate you to race where you once plodded.

BRAIN POWER DOUBLER #27

This is another exercise you can't afford to skip. Word-at-a-time reading is a basic stumbling block to faster reading.

1. Next time you read an article, book, or business document, look for the short phrases that contain a single idea.

2. Try to absorb them together, to take them in visually and mentally at the same time.

3. Press yourself through the material, identifying and going on to phrase after phrase. Don't linger to take in individual words, even if you are sure the process isn't working for you.

4. When you have finished, write a summary of all you remember.

5. Review the material. Once again, you may be startled to discover just how well phrase by phrase works.

6. Practice for several weeks or months, until it has become as much of a habit as word-by-word reading ever was.

Backtracking

Backtracking is the third of the three self-sabotaging habits that undermine our reading skills as adults. And of the three, backtracking may be the worst. Backtracking is when we go back over a word to make sure we saw it right. This is an almost universal trait. According to Michael McCarthy, backtracking is an unconscious habit that arises out of "our lack of confidence in our ability to understand the material. If we miss a word or a phrase, if our attention wanders for a moment, we instinctively feel that our comprehension will improve if we go back and read it again."

We're wrong to think this, however. Backtracking doesn't improve our understanding. It actually impairs our comprehension. Stopping at every word or phrase to go back over it interferes with the brain's ability to grasp the overall significance of what you are reading. It also disrupts our ability to follow how the details fit together.

Imagine an airplane being constructed like that. They screw in the first bolt. Then they have to unscrew it, take it out, and screw it back in before they can put in the second bolt. Then they have to take the second bolt back out, too, and put it back in before going on to screw in the third bolt and so on.

It would take twice as long to assemble the plane and be very frustrating besides. Now you have some idea of how much of your reading power is being drained off by the deceptively innocent act of backtracking.

BRAIN POWER DOUBLER #28

This is your chance to free yourself from the last reflex that holds your reading speed down to a fraction of its potential. Don't skip this exercise, either.

1. Select something lengthy to read.

2. Plow straight through it as fast as you can and don't let yourself stop to look at anything twice.

3. Again, when you are finished, write down what you remember. Compare that to what you read.

4. Press yourself to read this way until you feel it has become instinctive.

RETAINING WHAT YOU READ
WITH THE "READING REINFORCERS"

By now you should be reading many times faster than when you began this chapter and without any loss of comprehension. All the reading shortcuts in the world are worthless, however, unless you can remember and retain the key ideas from what you read. Yet nature would seem to have played a nasty trick on us here. Information we take in by reading, often precisely what we most want to remember, is the most difficult kind to recall.

Things we read make far less impact on us, and are therefore harder to remember, than are the happenings of the physical world around us. That's why most people have difficulty remembering something as simple as the title of a book they read, let alone the contents.

You've probably been called on the carpet some time in life—at work, in school, in the military, or during some other crucial endeavor—only to be quizzed about the details of a document you read only the day before. Suddenly your mind went blank. Or you discovered you had only a hazy memory of the contents.

Either way, the result was the same: You were humiliated, nervous, and came off looking bad. And you likely spent the next hour or so beating yourself up mentally for not being able to remember something you'd read such a short time earlier.

Yet, it wasn't your fault. If asked, you could have probably remembered what you had for dinner the night before and most of the details of the dinner conversation. Our interactions with the world around us are far more vivid, making a greater impact on memory, than are strings of black words printed on some piece of paper.

Ironically, it's what we take in through reading that is usually what we find ourselves needing to remember most. Almost everything important to our lives comes in printed form: corporate policy changes, employee handbooks, insurance policies, profit-and-loss forms. And you can fill in the blanks with your own experiences from there.

But this doesn't have to happen again. You can remember anything you read as clearly as the details of yesterday's dinner with the five "reading reinforcers."

Multiply your reading power with this simple five-step strategy. You will not only remember the details the next day, if quizzed, you'll retain them for a long time to come. The following reading reinforcers are five questions you should ask yourself after reading anything you want to recall later.

- ❏ What was it about?
- ❏ What was the most important information in it?
- ❏ What opinions, if any, did the writer present?
- ❏ What's your own opinion of it?
- ❏ What one element makes it unique?

BRAIN POWER DOUBLER #29

Never read anything important without engaging in this quick mental review afterward. In a sense, it is kin to the memory-retention systems we discussed in Part Two of this book. Next time you finish something you want to remember, ask yourself:

1. What was it about? (Notification of a new change in procedures for the sales staff, for example.)

2. What was the most important information in it? (Registers will no longer print out a paper copy of receipts for the store. They will print just one copy for the customer. The store receipt will be stored electronically via the department's LAN network.)

3. What opinions were presented in it, if any? (The new procedure would benefit everyone—store and employees. It would save time for them all by saving the step of putting the receipt in the cash drawer. It would also conserve resources by cutting the use of paper receipts by one half.)

4. What's your own opinion of it? (If there's ever a computer problem, we would be in big trouble. And we'd have no paper receipt we could re-create those figures from.)

5. What one element makes it unique? (I won't have to fool around with store receipts.)

Chapter 9

READING SMARTER

What if you could multiply your brain's reading power, not by double, but by ten times? What would that do for your work load, for your life, for the enrichment of your mind? This is one of the simplest chapters in this book, but you'll have multiplied your reading power ten times over when you finish it.

The fact is, too many people let the idea of reading intimidate them. They have the idea that reading is a chore. Because they approach it with this attitude, most people find reading difficult. So they put off reading. They let it pile up. The pile becomes ever larger. Soon they have fallen far behind and the prospect of reading all that stacked-up material becomes even more intimidating, seems only all that much more of a chore to get through.

Reading is a chore only when you don't know the smart way to read. Reading faster isn't the goal. It's reading smarter. The smarter, not harder, rule is one of life's cardinal principles. It's what took us from the cave to the central-heated and -cooled condo. It's behind every major advancement, from the wheel and the screw to the washing machine and the home PC.

"Smarter not harder" is what makes you suddenly turn off the freeway at 4 P.M. and take a back route home, just as rush-hour traffic is starting to build. "Smarter not harder" is the core of the concept of delegating authority. "Smarter not harder" is preparing five meals at once and freezing four for the future.

It's ubiquitous in almost everything you do. You may not have realized it was the principle at work. But "smarter not harder" underlies much, perhaps all, of human accomplishment.

It applies to reading, too. There are shortcuts you can use to double, triple, even quadruple the speed at which you zip through letters, books, reports, magazine articles, and the rest. And you won't have to learn a single so-called speed-reading technique.

According to Michael McCarthy, who teaches seminars in Active Reading, up to 90 percent of what we read is wasted effort. Most of it is off the main subject that interests us or it is literary flab. Only 10 percent, sometimes even less, actually contains information we can use.

How much time and effort could you save yourself if you could skip the 90 percent you don't need to know and go straight to the 10 percent you can use? You could read ten times as much in the same amount of time.

Where would the chore be in reading then? There'd be nothing intimidating or difficult about it. There'd be no reason to put it off because it would be over before you knew it.

Those piles of stacked-up reading you are behind on would melt like butter. Your eyes would flash right by all the irrelevant pages and words and zero in on the 5 or 10 or 20 items you actually need to read. Then you could put it aside, finished, and read the next item with the same quicksilver speed.

Reading researchers have targeted three miraculous strategies for bypassing what you don't need to know and going straight to the "meat"—the 10 percent that matters. They are

❑ Increasing your ideas per minute.

❑ Using the "reading map."

❑ Skimming.

INCREASE IPM (IDEAS PER MINUTE)— NOT WPM (WORDS PER MINUTE)

Robert R., the vice president of a large communications company, came to me. He had taken a famous speed-reading course. His reading rate was certifiably over 1,000 words per minute. Before, he had been overwhelmed with the amount of business correspondence, information, and trade journals he had to review each day. Although he was reading three times faster, he still couldn't get through it all, let alone through the peripherals such as his morning newspapers and several books he wanted to read. Robert actually felt farther behind than before he had taken the speed-reading course.

He had made a common mistake. He assumed that by reading faster, he was taking in information faster. That is only partly true. What Robert didn't realize was that, although he was reading faster, much of the material he was reading was irrelevant to his needs, repetitious, or otherwise a waste of his valuable time. Even after racing through hundreds of pages, he wasn't taking in much in the way of new ideas and crucial data. Robert had misplaced his focus. Rather than increasing the number of words he was taking in, he should have been concentrating on the amount of vital information he was absorbing.

Many people mistakenly focus on increasing the speed at which they take in words. They've been dazzled by the claims of speed-reading seminars that promise rates such as 2,000 words per minute and reading whole pages at a glance. But taking in more words faster isn't the reason you are reading. It's acquiring important facts and ideas.

It's not increasing your WPM (words per minute) that counts when you are trying to keep abreast of the information flood. More words per minute won't get you where you want to go, especially when many of those words don't concern what you want to know. Reading them won't get you any closer to your goal. It's your IPM (ideas per minute) rate that you should be striving to increase.

Focusing on reading speed fools you into misdirecting your efforts toward plowing through mountains of irrelevant and unnecessary words. You can take in all an author's ideas without reading all her or his words. The heading for this section, for instance, or almost any one of the sentences in it could give you a sense of the key points.

There's another benefit to reading for ideas. You are far more likely to focus on and remember what you learn. Singling out the main ideas in what you read won't be difficult.

I gave Robert the following exercise: It helped him increase his IPM and zip through the piles of reading required to keep up with an ever-changing communications industry.

BRAIN DOUBLER #30

Practice this next time you read a newspaper, magazine, or anything that takes about 30 minutes. It requires reading material, a timer, and something to write on. You'll learn to zero in on the important ideas instantly and effortlessly.

1. Set a timer for 15 minutes.

2. Read at your normal speed.

3. Stop reading and write down what you remember as the key ideas.

4. Reset the timer for the same amount of time.

5. Resume reading. But this time try to speed through and jump past anything that doesn't look like an idea. You'll have to glance through it all. But do just that—glance at it. Don't bother to take in every word and detail. Stop and read carefully anytime you find material that seems as if it might be germane to your own needs or might contain key ideas.

6. If it does contain important information, read it at your normal pace.

7. If it doesn't, then speed on. Look for material that seems worth noting.

8. Stop reading and again write down what you remember as the key ideas.

9. Compare the number of ideas you took in the first time with the number you took in during your second reading session. You are likely to be surprised at the result. (With practice you can easily multiply that number exponentially.)

TAKE TIME-SAVING SHORTCUTS WITH THE "READING MAP"

Most people unknowingly waste a lot of unnecessary reading time because they don't know a simple secret: The vast majority of fact-based journals, articles, reports, and books are written around a universal template or map.

Just like a road map, you can get to your destination faster, locate important stops, avoid dead-ends, use shortcuts, and have an all-around more pleasant time when you base your course on a "reading map." It will help you locate the precise information you want up to 98 percent more quickly.

The reading map is based on the simple premise that most factual material is constructed according to well-known, classical principles:

❑ A main theme (main point)

❑ Supportive material

❑ Subthemes (subsidiary points)

❑ Supportive material

❑ Sub-subthemes

❑ Supportive material

Paragraphs, subsections, sections, chapters, and books all follow this format. Each elaborates one main idea or image. The opening of each states the theme. The body contains the supporting materials. The end sums up the point being made or elaborates on its significance.

In the case of a book or detailed report, there can be a large number of subsidiary points. This can even turn into what the author of *How to Be Twice as Smart* describes as a kind of "infinite regression of subthemes, sub-subthemes, sub-sub-subthemes, and so on."

Each theme or point is in turn supported by illustrative, explanatory, or substantiating material. This can include everything from facts and figures to clarifications, case histories, examples, descriptions, and definitions—even photographs, illustrations, diagrams, tables, graphs, tables, and charts.

Brain Power Doubler #31

Next time you have an important report, manual, stack of correspondence, or book to read, follow these steps.

1. Go through it quickly, reading only the headings and subheadings. See how many of the key ideas and how much of the general thrust of the material you can glean from this alone.

2. Ask yourself which headings seem to indicate the material that will contain the information of greatest interest to you.

3. Now go back and read just those sections.

4. Roughly calculate how much of the report, article, or book you didn't read. Is it 10, 20, even 50 percent, or more?

5. Imagine how much more you could read if you saved only that same percentage of your reading time every time you read.

SKIPPING "PLACE HOLDERS"—THE FINE ART OF SKIMMING

Here's the ultimate refinement of the reading map. Now that you know what you are looking for, you're going to learn four powerful tools for identifying and zigzagging past all the material in a publication or abstract that's garbage as far as you are concerned. Reading research has revealed another surprising statistic: As much as 20 percent to 50 percent of reading matter is taken up with meaningless "place holders." Place holders are connective or illustrative phrases, paragraphs, and even pages that are necessary for writing to be technically correct and help slower readers get the point. Place holders serve a variety of functions.

❑ They connect ideas.

❑ They make transitions between subjects.

❑ They illustrate points already made.

❑ They cite journals and books the author consulted.

❑ They repeat what has already been said for inattentive readers.

The one thing place holders don't do is contain valuable ideas or information. As far as content goes, they are null and void. Eliminate all the place holders from reading material, and the key ideas and information would still be there.

Every minute you spend reading place holders is an irreplaceable minute of your life—and valuable reading time—lost. But you can learn to recognize and skip place holders in fractions of a second while skimming over the rest. You already know how to skim. Everyone does it. But with the reading map to guide you and with a few little insider tricks, you can skim so quickly and accurately you'll find yourself absorbing pages worth of information in just a minute or two. The following four shortcuts will show you how to skim through anything lengthy from manuals and reports to entire books, catching everything important, in virtually no time.

❑ Don't get bogged down in details.

❑ Skip what you don't need to know.

❑ Let the writers identify key ideas for you.

❑ Find the topic sentence.

❑ Watch for signposts that signal a change of subject.

Don't Get Bogged Down in Details

It isn't the details you want, it's the main point or idea. Most printed material was written to make a point. The details are merely there to illustrate the point. Often you are reading to find that point or a series of points. That's all you need to know. The specific details that lead to it are irrelevant.

In that case, you are home free. Just look for key words related to your area or areas of interest. If it's articles in tennis magazines related to injuries, key words might be "doctor," "accident," "injury," "collision," and so forth.

Or say you're looking for the exact figures on U.S. semiconductor sales in 1995 in an article about general trends in the field over the last decade and a half. Scan down the page looking for the numeral "1995." When you see it, briefly dip into the material that follows. If it contains the sales information you need, you've hit paydirt.

Brain Power Doubler #32

Use this approach when it's the document's or publication's main point or points you are seeking.

1. Focus in on precisely what kind of material you are interested in reading about.

2. Select one to six key words that are likely to appear in any discussion of it.

3. Let your eye run quickly down the page, reading the center couple of words in each line, looking for phrases that tip off that the point you are looking for might be contained there.

4. Any time you detect them, slow down and read the surrounding material.

Skip What You Don't Need to Know

Sometimes you do need to know details. But it probably isn't all the details, just the ones pertaining to certain topics. Much—sometimes most—of the material in a document isn't on the subject you are interested in. Only certain portions deal with aspects that are directly of concern to you. Whether it's two thirds or one tenth, you should skip it, too. Instead, concentrate on locating and reading the sections that pertain. The time you save will be your own.

For example, most reports, analyses, letters, abstracts, books, and magazine and newspaper articles begin with a few lines or paragraphs summarizing their basic theme and general content. So do most chapters, sections, and subsections. A quick peek at the start of each will tell you if, and where, material of interest to you can be found. If there is nothing of interest, on to the next.

When the main ideas aren't summarized at the beginning, they are almost always recapped at the end. For example, if you were a busy businesswoman reading an article in *Forbes* rating the top 25 mutual funds and you were looking to invest your money in the number-one fund, the details wouldn't concern you. All you would want to know would be which mutual fund number one is. Most of the article would be detailed specifics of each fund's operations and productivity. You could skim the opening paragraphs to see if the article opened with the top fund or with number 25. Then you could skip to the opening or end of the article and read the number-one fund's name and call your broker.

BRAIN POWER DOUBLER #33

This four-step technique is ideal when you are reading for specific information.

1. Start reading.
2. Start at the beginning. See if the key ideas are stated there.
3. If not, take a peek at the end. You'll probably find them there.
4. Repeat this process as often as necessary until you reach the end.

Let the Writers Identify Key Ideas for You

These days, you don't have to look for key ideas. The people who write books, magazines, brochures, reports, and the like do the work of identifying key ideas and important changes of subject for you.

Nearly all published material today has capitalized headings that come between some paragraphs to indicate when a new theme or subtheme is being discussed. These headings encapsulate the point of the material that follows. You've seen them in newspapers, books, reports, literally everywhere.

Writers also employ other typographical tricks, such as italics, boldface, underlining, numbered lists, charts, and change of font to make important facts or crucial ideas stand out above the rest (much as I have done in this book).

In most cases, zeroing in on the 10 percent you need to read is, literally, as simple as casting your eye upon the page. You'll find the main points leaping out and drawing your attention to them.

BRAIN POWER DOUBLER #34

Use this when you need to review great piles of research books and documents for a few key facts or categories. You'll find everything you want while sailing through them with amazing speed and ease.

1. Place all the material you have to go through before you on a desk or beside a comfortable chair.

2. One at a time, leaf through their pages. Ignore all the material set in regular type. Scan only for words and phrases set in type that looks different. When you encounter any that seem to apply to your areas of interest, slow down and read more carefully.

3. Repeat this process until you are finished.

Find the Topic Sentence

When typography has led you to an interesting section or when there are no headings to help guide you, look for the topic sentence. Most well-written paragraphs contain one important sentence that sums up the content of the entire paragraph. This is the topic sentence. Often (but not always) the topic sentence will be the first sentence in the paragraph.

In the previous sections, two of the topic sentences are "It isn't the details you want, it's the main point or idea" and "Much—sometimes most—of the material in a document isn't on the subject you are interested in."

Topic sentences make locating the passages that interest you that much easier. With a little practice, you'll learn to spot them at a glance.

Brain Power Doubler #35

Spotting topic sentences is a simple matter. Try these steps when you need to find very specific information within short articles, material without headings, or within a larger section in books and long documents.

1. Scan the first sentence of each paragraph.

2. Ignore those that seem to center around specific details.

3. Look for a sentence that seems to offer a general statement relating to your subject, such as a general trend or a summation or import of a larger body of information.

Watch for Signposts That Signal a Change of Subject

You don't even have to read every topic sentence. Merely by running your eye down the left-hand side of the page, you can spot most important changes of subject.

Certain words signal that a new idea is about to be introduced or that crucial supportive material is about to follow. Typically such words come at the beginning of paragraphs, where they are easy to spot.

These verbal signposts include "But," "However," "On the other hand," "Always," "Although," "When," "If," "Necessarily," "In short," and "In fact," among others. When you see one, take a second look. The new subject it signals might be just what you are interested in.

BRAIN POWER DOUBLER #36

The following can save your life when you have to find something very specific in a long document and have very little time to do it.

1. Look for the verbal signposts given in the previous section.

2. When you see one, slow down. It's a sign that a new theme or subject is about to come up.

3. As always, when skimming, take a second glance through the material. If there is nothing of interest, skim on.

Chapter 10

EVALUATING
WHAT YOU READ

You've doubled your brain power by reading smarter and faster. Now go for a grand slam. Double it again by learning to separate the printed wheat from the chaff, almost instantly. Just zipping through all the printed data that are thrown at you every day isn't enough. There's another step left. It will take you from mere mastery of quantity to mastery of quality.

In the late 1980s, Ruth J., a friend who had just received a rather large inheritance in the 1.5-million-dollar range, stumbled on what looked like a great investment opportunity. The owner of a small software firm with a best-selling DOS accounting program was seeking a partner with working capital to help tide the company through a financial crunch. The company itself was healthy, he told Ruth. The current crisis was the result of a distributor who had gone bankrupt while owing the software firm nearly a million dollars.

Ruth was no fool. She did her homework—or thought she did—and the president of the company appeared to do everything to help her. He provided her the previous year's annual company report, and Ruth read through every word. It was filled with glowing accounts of the firm's past success and the company's prospects. It pointed out that successful software brand names were like successful breakfast cereal names: Once the public found one they liked, they kept coming back to it. The sales figures in the report bore out this premise. To prove his product's quality, the company president gave Ruth the names of several leading software designers, and all confirmed that it would remain far ahead of other DOS accounting systems for years to come. Ruth was convinced. She invested her inheritance. And lost it! Less than 18 months later, the software maker was belly-up. DOS software was on the way out; Bill Gates's Windows had eclipsed it.

What went wrong? Ruth reviewed all the relevant information, didn't she? It wasn't the quantity of what she read that was the problem. It was the quality. She had missed the last—and most vital—step in reading. She had read uncritically. She had neglected to question or evaluate what she read. Among the other mistakes she had made were not considering the source of information (the company needed her investment to continue operating; naturally, they painted the best possible picture); relying on vague generalizations (those glowing accounts of the company's future omitted all word of Windows); relying on argument by analogy (cornflakes can't be superseded by a new technology overnight); relying on out-of-date information (the previous year's report); and being impressed by authorities who really weren't (the software programmers knew about the quality of the product, but not about the way consumer psychology would bring Windows to the top).

Simply taking in mountains of knowledge uncritically isn't enough. Unfortunately, not all the things we learn and see and hear can be believed. Among the avalanche of facts, figures, and ideas we are exposed to there is much bogus information. We are bombarded by much that is neither factual, accurate, unbiased, nor even truthful.

In a world where success depends on keeping abreast of so unprecedented an information explosion, mistakenly acting on bad data can be disastrous. This is true at every level of our lives. From business to career to the intimately personal, making the right decision depends on getting the right facts and the facts right.

Information can easily become contaminated, sometimes innocently, sometimes with more ulterior motives in mind. Either way, the result is the same for us. We can be cheated, manipulated, misled, or dangerously misinformed.

According to Scott Witt, a successful entrepreneur and author of books on business and personal success, bogus data can become bogus in several ways:

- Facts from people who have a personal stake in the matter
- Observations of people who have little training or experience in that particular field
- Hastily prepared data that may have typographical or numerical errors
- Superficial reports that don't go thoroughly into the subject

❏ Preconceived notions that were never right in the first place

❏ Or, it can simply be out-of-date

Just think about it. We all know someone who started his or her own business with high hopes, only to have it fail due to bad advice or a misunderstanding of critical details. Most of us have been deliberately taken advantage of in some way by an unscrupulous individual or company that deliberately misled and deceived us. Some of us have made a key decision and later found, to our regret, that it was based on out-of-date information.

A cardinal rule of the information age is never accept anything uncritically. That only leads to disaster. Be sure what you absorb is accurate and current before acting on it. Otherwise, it's worse than useless—it's harmful. Separating the informational wheat from the chaff is the all-important step. It's what distinguishes an excellent learner from a master of the information flow. It's also not very hard.

Fourteen proven tools will show you how to detect what's bogus as soon as it's presented. You'll be able to evaluate the material's worth—and more important, its lack of worth—almost instantly in most cases. In short, you have mastered both the quantity of information flooding into your life and have assured its quality. What once seemed an insurmountable mountain of information will now seem like the proverbial molehill.

SEVEN SURE-FIRE WAYS TO SPOT BOGUS, ERRONEOUS, AND DISTORTED INFORMATION

In most cases, determining the validity of what you read and hear isn't a lengthy or difficult process. You don't have to pull down research books or look it up somewhere. You can tell good from bad at first glance. Any time you're exposed to new ideas or data, ask yourself the following questions. They will help you spot the bad stuff (BS) 90 percent of the time, without any further effort being necessary. Ask yourself:

❏ Are there undefined terms or ambiguous language?

❏ What is the source of information?

❏ Do any statements contain generalizations?

☐ Does it rely primarily on analogy?

☐ Is it current?

☐ Is it firsthand or secondhand?

☐ Is there supporting evidence or is it just a point of view?

Are There Undefined Words or Ambiguous Language?

Genuine information is always presented in concrete words and figures. Look for vague language and ambiguous words that are open to interpretation, particularly those that might be interpreted in more than one way.

BRAIN POWER DOUBLER #37

Here are some red flags that signal us the material that follows may not be as reliable as it seems: "many," "the majority," "market forces," "experts say," "everyone," "justice," "liberal," "conservative." Also be careful when technical or unusual words are left undefined. You can't evaluate something if you don't know what parts of it mean.

What Is the Source of Information?

Sometimes a speaker's or a writer's sources of information are inadequate, faulty, or plain wrong. Never rely on facts if their source is not clearly stated. If the attribution is vague or nonexistent, you are right to reject or mistrust the material.

BRAIN POWER DOUBLER #38

Look for these signposts: "experts," "informed sources," "a national publication," "a television news broadcast," "a scholarly journal" and others. If no source is given, be doubly suspicious.

Do Any Statements Contain Generalizations?

Distrust generalizations, along with ideas or arguments based on them. Categorical statements about groups or individuals are rarely valid. Life comes in too many varieties. Nothing is true for everyone.

> ### Brain Power Doubler #39
>
> Watch for generalities such as, "politicians are spend-crazy," "venture capitalists bail out at the first sign of trouble," "workers aren't as loyal as they used to be," "corporations are soulless," "lawyers are crooks," "'their kind' are lazy. "If you can add the word "all" to a phrase ("all workers . . . ," "all politicians . . . ," "all women . . .") it's a generalization you can easily dismiss.

Does It Rely Primarily on Analogy?

Analogy is notoriously unreliable. Analogies are ways of illustrating points or issues by comparing them to something with similar characteristics. It assumes that because there is a relationship between two things, they must therefore be alike in every way. But different things are never completely comparable; they always diverge somewhere, in some fashion. Running a business might, in many ways, be like a medieval Japanese Samurai swordfight. But it isn't a swordfight, and it could be dangerous to make business decisions solely according to the principles of ancient Bushido.

> ### Brain Power Doubler #40
>
> Be wary of actions, proofs, and conclusions that spring from analogy alone.

Is It Current?

Things change, circumstances alter, new technologies and ideas supersede one another with lightning rapidity in our modern age. When a fact or figure is not current, it may well be wrong. The older it is, the more likely is the information to be out of date.

> ### Brain Power Doubler #41
>
> If a citation is more than a few years old (a few months in fast-breaking fields such as computers), you have good cause to be careful. Log on or drop into a bookstore or library and see what the newest publications in that field have to say.

Is It Firsthand or Secondhand?

The best information comes firsthand from those who actually know whereof they speak. As with gossip, the more people it passes through on its way to you, the greater the opportunity for intentional or unintentional error. Newspapers and general-circulation magazines usually get their facts from reading books by experts or interviewing experts (who are often misquoted). An article based on a newspaper or magazine account adds yet one more likelihood that what's being said could be seriously flawed. So can a fact repeated second, third, or fourth-hand—or even worse—by any speaker.

BRAIN POWER DOUBLER #42

When the currency of information is a critical factor, don't accept it at face value. Take the time to locate the original person or study (libraries and the Internet are great for this), and make sure what you have been told by others is correct.

Is There Supporting Evidence or Is It Just a Point of View?

One drawback of the electronic age is that we are barraged on all fronts by personal points of view masquerading as facts. It's just personal opinion unless the author or speaker offers specific figures, surveys, sources, or actual cases. Anything else is unsupported assumptions. Without expertise or verifiable data, one person's opinion is no better than any other's. Points of view can be enlightening, but don't mistake them for facts.

BRAIN POWER DOUBLER #43

It's poor judgment to proceed on the basis of nothing more substantial than someone else's personal opinion.

SPOTTING "INFORMATION MANIPULATION"

In 95 percent of all cases when you find something worth noting, remembering, or acting on, the previous seven questions will tell you if it's bogus or not. But some writers, authors, and speakers are experts at massaging facts and slanting words to create misleading conclusions and have hidden agendas. But you can unmask their efforts to bamboozle, mislead, and exploit you. It's easy to spot such information manipulation every time when you know the telltale clues.

❑ Spotting "Selected Proofs"

❑ Spotting "Red Herrings"

❑ Spotting "Mudslinging"

❑ Spotting "Emotionally Loaded Arguments"

❑ Spotting "Appeals to Authority"

❑ Spotting "Faulty Conclusions Based on Flawed Arguments"

My friend, Dr. Samantha N., a general practitioner, faced a mountain of mailers from pharmaceutical companies every day. Each touted the benefits of its medicines and drugs. Medical school had trained her to heal. But not a word was said about how to evaluate the sales pitches of drug companies. Samantha left one of my California seminars armed with the knowledge of how to spot information manipulation. Three weeks later, she called to report that the knowledge allowed her to identify phony claims and dubious products. Once she had started to do that, Samantha said, she noticed that some companies were more deceptive in the way they presented their facts than others. She planned to scrutinize any medicine that came from their laboratories very carefully before using it.

Spotting "Selected Proofs"

Information manipulators are masters at presenting only material that supports their ideas. They deliberately leave out all the inconvenient facts that contradict them. (And since there are two sides to every story, there is always something to be said for the other side.) For example, what if someone wanted to sell you on the effectiveness of their management-training seminar? The brochure would be filled with glowing testimonials from those who had great success putting the seminars' principles into practice. It would look worthwhile. But those individuals might number only a few out of hundreds or thousands. Many more might have had just the opposite experience; they might have found that what the seminar taught didn't work in real life. (And those who did succeed might well have succeeded because of their own talent, in spite of the seminar, not because of it.)

Brain Power Doubler #44

Always assume there is another side to the story. Look for it and you'll find it.

Spotting "Red Herrings"

Information manipulators try to distract you from finding holes in their argument or asking logical questions about some of their statements that might otherwise arise in your mind. Some people call these "informational red-herrings." The proverbial example is the speaker who has been asked an embarrassing question and must change the subject because he does not dare answer it. "We all agree that company earnings could have been better this year. But to raise questions of mismanagement is extreme. After all, many other businesses experienced a downturn. The economic picture, as you all know . . ."

Brain Power Doubler #45

When someone suddenly raises an issue that seems unrelated to the main subject, he or she is trying to throw you off the track. Be wary of all that follows.

Spotting "Mudslinging"

When the going gets rough, information manipulators get rougher. If they can't substantiate their position, or if a rival's is better, they ignore the issues and start slinging mud at the other person. A salesperson making a presentation to an important client might seek to dismiss a question from a rival salesperson on the grounds that the other has a mercenary motivation in asking it. While it might be true that the person asking has a personal interest in the matter, his or her point might still be valid.

BRAIN POWER DOUBLER #46

When you spot mudslinging, watch out! There is something the mudslinger doesn't want you to know.

Spotting "Emotionally Loaded Arguments"

Information manipulators are also expert at stirring up emotion to enlist us in a cause or to turn us against one. Words don't just convey facts. They also convey feelings. No one likes to be called "stupid." It arouses feelings of anger. The words "injured child" are likely to evoke strong emotions in most people. When someone wants to turn off your critical faculties so you will miss important holes in their contentions, they sprinkle what they have to say liberally with emotionally laden appeals. Hearing a "defeatist attitude is undermining the whole company's position" is very upsetting. But is it true, or is the person making the accusation just trying to cover up his or her own substandard performance?

BRAIN POWER DOUBLER #47

When you spot emotionally laden arguments, ignore them. Look elsewhere for the truth.

Spotting "Appeals to Authority"

Information manipulators love to dazzle you with endorsements from celebrities and experts. "Professor Schmitz of Harvard takes the same position," an information manipulator might say. But a professor of marketing may not always know what works in practice. Furthermore, the experts are sometimes wrong. More important, people sometimes get the authorities they quote wrong. Sometimes they even get them completely reversed.

BRAIN POWER DOUBLER #48

When an argument rests entirely on the say-so of some eminent authority, things are getting tenuous. Go slowly, be skeptical. You are probably treading informational quicksand.

Spotting Faulty Conclusions Based On Flawed Arguments

What information manipulators are leading up to with all this is false conclusions based on faulty facts and flawed arguments. The whole idea is to distract you thoroughly from gaping weaknesses in their own position by stirring up your emotions with smear campaigns, words, and appeals to authority. These are common strategies in sales, politics, and advertising. The software company looked like such an attractive investment to Ruth because faulty evidence had deliberately been manipulated to create a false picture of the company's potential.

BRAIN POWER DOUBLER #49

The more BS busters you spot while reading, the more carefully you want to scrutinize the conclusions. Most of the time you'll find there is misrepresentation somewhere.

WHEN IN DOUBT, CHECK!

There are no unimpeachable sources. According to newspaper reports, several years back a businessman almost made a fatal decision based on figures given in the annual *Statistical Abstract of the United States*. This important document contains the key national population and other demographic statistics used by business and governmental bodies. It is published by the U.S. government printing office. By pure luck, the businessman discovered that there was an error of a decimal place in the stats on certain kinds of plastic production. Further research, widely reported, discovered this vital book was riddled with hundreds of errors, major and minor.

You don't have to rely on luck to save you, however. With the BS Detectors you've acquired, you will be able to discern the authentic from the bogus in all but a few instances. When it's business, when the information is critical, double-check. Make that visit to the library, tap into the World Wide Web, ask a friend or a friend's friend who is an expert.

Brain Power Doubler #50

Almost any fact, figure, name, or data you could ever want to know is easily accessible due to computers and data links, and most city libraries now have computers that can do quick searches for you. The year's soybean crop, the number of rainy days in Iowa City, how much is spent on print advertising in Norfolk, Virginia—it's all no more than 20 seconds to 20 minutes away.

The information age may present many demands. But it also provides many opportunities. Now that you have the tools and abilities to manage both the quantity and the quality of the information flowing into your life, you are free to use as powerful aids the same computers, faxes, cable channels, modems, and other tools that once threatened to overwhelm you. These fabulous new channels of information flow two ways—from them to you and from you to them. Take advantage of them, and you can literally have precisely the information you want, when you want it, delivered right to your fingertips. Conquering the information age couldn't be easier.

DOUBLING YOUR
LISTENING POWER

Chapter 11

INSTANT LISTENING

Do you know what's the fastest growing area of the publishing industry? Audio books! Work, leisure, and family life make so many demands on us these days, we often come up short on reading time. But increasingly, statistics show, we spend a half hour every morning and evening commuting to and from our workplaces to our homes. Stuck in the car, with all that time on our hands, many of us are turning to audio books that allow us to make the most of the hours we spend traveling. (Via pocket-sized tape players, those who ride both ways on mass transit, as well as joggers, bicyclists, and others are making use of what might otherwise be lost time via instructional, inspirational, and educational audios.)

The one drawback with most approaches to increasing brain power is that they place their focus almost entirely on reading. Yet statistics, and a bit of thought, show that we take in three times as much information through listening—meetings, lectures, conversations, radio, television, audio tapes, and so forth—as through reading. There's no point in devoting all your energy to boosting your reading power when the same effort applied to listening would multiply your brain power by 300 percent.

What few people realize is that failure to be a good listener prevents us from hearing and retaining vital information, becoming a roadblock to personal and professional success. Our relations with loved ones depend on hearing their needs, whether expressed directly in words or more subtly in tones and partial hints. Business is little more than a constant ebb and flow of conversations, phone calls, instructions, meetings, presentations, and demonstrations, all conducted via the spoken word.

So what's the big deal about listening? You already shut your mouth and concentrate attentively. What more could be involved? Naturally, you are already listening when other people talk. But do you listen well? Do you hear everything that is being said? Do you understand it completely?

Contrary to popular opinion, being a good listener requires much more than just keeping quiet while the other person talks. Listening well is a difficult art. You'll comprehend just how difficult if you try to repeat accurately the key points of a detailed conversation or lecture just an hour afterward.

Archie Goodwin, the narrator second-hero of the celebrated Nero Wolfe mystery series, was a typical tough-guy detective, with a difference. The redoubtable Mr. Goodwin had trained himself to be able to repeat verbatim every single world of every conversation he heard, complete with inflection. This turned out to be a valuable trait to his employer, the reclusive Nero Wolfe, who never left his brownstone on a case, relying on Goodwin to visit the crime scene and act as a human tape recorder for him.

Most of us have wished we possessed Archie Goodwin's special talent. Who wouldn't like to multiply his or her listening power and remember every word a superior, colleague, client, lecturer, or lover said? What a boost that would be in your brain power. What an edge that would give you in life.

Fortunately, Archie Goodwin's abilities aren't unique to fiction. Anyone can acquire them. Researchers such as professor of psychology J. J. Allen have been studying for years how we can listen more effectively. They have found that to become an effective listener, we need to

❏ Overcome bad mental habits that prevent us from listening closely.

❏ Become personally absorbed in what is being said.

❏ Pinpoint the main idea.

❏ Take care not to react too fast or draw conclusions too quickly.

❏ Evaluate the speaker's expertise.

❏ Determine how much weight should be given to the speaker's words.

This chapter and the two that follow focus on strategies and exercises that will dramatically increase your ability to pay attention to, understand, and remember what you hear. To become, in short, an instant listener.

GENERATING PERSONAL INTEREST

Whitley just had to pass his bar exam; he had already flunked it two years before. There was a cushy position waiting for him with his father, who headed a highly successful personal injury practice. Until then, Whitley was on a bare-bones allowance for punishment and had to drop his membership at the health club, stop charging expensive Armani suits, and engage in other frugalities.

How Whitley had passed law school, I never completely understood. Whitley had no interest in law or in becoming an attorney. He really wanted to get involved in venture capital—rolling out small, new high-tech companies and other entrepreneurial activities.

To ensure Whitley did well on his bar exams, his father sent him to a special workshop the weekend before the exams. There he heard one lecturer and presentation after another refresh the audience on the essentials they needed to know to pass the exams. Whitley did his best to concentrate on every word, knowing how much depended on it.

But when the time came to take the exams, it was the same old story. Whitley flunked again. "I tried," he told me tearfully later. "I really tried to focus on all that boring stuff about torts and injuries and the 'deep pockets' law. But somehow it was all gone when I sat down to take the exams."

In one form or another, and to a greater or lesser degree, the same thing has happened to us all. We listen to an important presentation or view a video about a subject that we aren't interested in or are certain will be dull. Despite our best efforts to absorb and retain it all, when the critical moment comes we can't remember a single word and have only the haziest grasp of what was said.

Contrast that situation with one in which someone was extremely cruel to you—even as far back as childhood—yet you remember almost every word. Or take another example; most people remember verbatim what they said when they promised themselves to their spouse or were proposed to. Or that one time you got out a great line in response to an insult and were able to repeat it word for word to entertain friends for years afterward. Or the time that NFL champion personally described his league-winning touchdown to you—you probably still remember every word.

What makes the difference? In all the cases in which you could still vividly recall the speaker's words, you had a personal stake or interest in what was being said. As with the other forms of brain power, the key to multiplying your listening power is personal involvement.

Of course, personal involvement is already there when you're listening to something absorbing. But what about stuff that's boring? How do you generate the kind of personal involvement that will burn words into your memory when people are droning out dry facts and figures or when the subject at hand leaves you cold?

Well, as G. K. Chesterton once said, "There is no such thing as an uninteresting subject; there are only uninterested people." Every subject has some interesting angle, and every subject has some impact on your life. The challenge is to search out those elements; after that you won't need to worry about forgetting what is being said. You'll be hanging on every word.

Generating personal involvement like this is easier than you might think. In researching what motivates us to listen well, psychologists Mihaly Csikszentmihalyi and Dominick A. Barbara have stumbled across an almost magical formula anyone can use to turn what you might have once thought "uninteresting dross" into "listening gold." When what's being discussed seems boring or involving, the following steps are guaranteed to help you locate the vital personal connection to the subject at hand.

❐ Abandon your prejudices that certain subjects are boring.

❐ Search out what has impact on your life or could prove of value to you; it's there, and you will find it.

The next exercise shows how these principles can generate excitement and involvement no matter how dull the speaker or subject.

Brain Power Doubler #51

Use this strategy to heighten your listening power by getting involved and staying in tune with what is being said at meetings, seminars, even casual conversations.

1. Abandon your prejudices that certain subjects are dull, uninspiring, or of no interest to you. (I pointed out to Whitley that his belief that personal injury law was boring and had no relevance to his future in venture capital had prevented him from hearing critical facts related to the profession he really wanted to pursue.)

2. Listen for elements that impact on your own areas of interest or future plans. (Had Whitley not made up his mind in advance, he might have realized that a large personal injury settlement or a class-action personal injury suit could bankrupt a small, tightly financed company unless the company was extremely well insured. Closer attention to what was said at the seminar would have told him how much of a threat such suits might pose and how to best prepare for or prevent them if he did become involved in financing a new venture.)

ENLISTING MENTAL INVOLVEMENT

How much of what you hear during the course of a day can you actively recall by its end, or by the next morning? Here's an instant mental review that will supply the answer: Write down everything you remember of what was said to you between yesterday morning and noon.

Unless you are an exceptional person, you might have been able to remember most of the highlights but not all the hundreds of details. Why not? The answer may surprise you. Most people would say it's because people talk too fast and they can't slow things down so they can focus on the details "like you can when you read a book."

Unfortunately, scientific research tells us the opposite is true. Most people talk at about 150 words per minute. A fast talker does about 200 WPM. But your brain can interpret and understand some

500 words per minute, which means you have plenty of time to absorb each word (even time to think two thoughts in between each word). More astonishingly, most of us read at about 350 to 500 words per minute, considerably faster than people speak.

So why can't we remember very well what we hear? Primarily, because we don't pay close attention to what we are hearing. The act of reading involves concentrating on each individual word, its meaning and the larger meaning it makes up in combination with the words on both sides. Naturally, what we read impresses itself deeply on the mind.

If we listened as actively as we read, we would retain far more of what we hear. But most of us listen passively. We just let the words flow in one ear and, not surprisingly, they tend to flow out the other.

We approach listening as if we were a sponge and expected our brains to somehow absorb the words for us. It never seems to occur to us that the only way we are going to "bring home the bacon" mentally is to set our minds to work—and keep them working—actively tuning in on every word that is spoken. But only when we actively follow the speakers' words, thoughts, and meaning can we truly say we are "listening" to them.

Use any of the following six techniques for getting your mind actively involved in "tuning in" on what is being said. Any one of them alone would double your brain power. Employ all six and you won't just become a "good" listener, you'll be a "super" listener.

- ❑ Listen actively; passive listening allows what you hear to go in one ear and out the other.

- ❑ Ask yourself what the speaker is trying to say; it will keep you thinking about what you are hearing.

- ❑ Listen with your feelings; they can respond to clues your conscious mind missed.

- ❑ Keep asking yourself if you understand what is being said; when you miss key points you understand less and less of what follows.

- ❑ Listen for something you can offer an intelligent comment on; the personal interaction gets you more involved.

- ❑ Ignore distractions. Letting your attention be drawn to trivialities like a speaker's appearance, random noises, an uncomfortable chair, even a toothache can result in missing critical information.

Listen Actively

There's more to listening than just passively hearing the words someone is speaking. A tape recorder could do that. One way to make certain you are consciously focused on what the speaker is saying is to try to "fill in the blanks" by anticipating what you think the speaker will say next. This will keep you mentally involved, thinking and actively listening.

Ask Yourself What the Speaker Is Trying to Say

Only 10 percent of what most speakers say is crucial; the rest is illustrative anecdotes, attempts at humor, additional explanation, and transitions from one topic to another. The mind responds most fully to what is most important. Focus on the part that's crucial, the basic message at any particular point. Try constantly to restate in your own terms what the person is saying. Consciously take the time to think to yourself, "What I think the speaker means here is . . ." Analyze the logic of the sentences, the choice of words, the facts presented. What is their overall point? Once you understand the essence, the details will make sense and you will know how to respond.

Listen With Your Feelings

Don't listen just with your intellect. Your feelings count. They come from the deep unconscious, where subtle cues you can miss with your conscious mind are totaled up below the level of consciousness. Feelings can tell you as much as thought. When you feel good or bad about a speaker or something he or she has said, it's a clue that your unconscious has put two and two together and come up with a positive evaluation or a negative one.

Understand What Is Being Said or Get Clarification

When we don't understand what is being said, our minds become restless and bored; listening power takes a nose dive. Keep asking yourself throughout if you understand what is being said. If you can't clearly state the speaker's point in your own terms, something is amiss. Either you have failed to understand what was said, or the speaker did not express himself or herself fully enough. When this happens, don't hesitate. If circumstances permit, ask for clarification. And keep asking until you are sure you fully understand. Don't settle for comprehending only half and pretending you comprehend it all just because you don't want to take up too much time.

Offer an Intelligent Comment

To keep your active attention on what is being said, get involved in the proceedings. When the situation permits it, offer your own perspective on what is being said. Whenever some statement or statistic sets off a related train of thought or cuts across one of your own areas of expertise, share your thoughts or viewpoint. Add supporting material, correct a misstatement, offer a different point of view. The interaction with the speaker, as well as with other listeners, will generate mental interest.

Ignore Distractions

Every situation in which someone is speaking is rife with potential distractions. It could be too hot or too cold, the audience might be restless and noisy, there could be annoying sounds from workmen in an adjoining room. Speakers themselves are often sources of distraction: They have annoying physical mannerisms such as coughs, tics, restless movement, mumbling, uninspiring delivery, an off-putting appearance, and many more. But each time you allow distractions to divert your mind from what is being said, you halve your listening power. Let distraction come between you and the message long enough and your recall of what is said will be almost nil.

BRAIN POWER DOUBLER #52

Walk away from that sales meeting, that management seminar, that impromptu budget discussion, that political stump speech with everything important locked in your mind. Enlist your own mental involvement with these six steps, each warranted to turn you from a passive to an active listener. From now on, when you find yourself listening to something important:

1. Listen actively. Try to "fill in the blanks" by anticipating what the speaker will say next. (If the speaker has been detailing statistics linking cigarette smoking to lung cancer and emphysema, how might you anticipate the following sentence would end? "The single greatest preventable cause of death in the United States is ____.")

Brain Power Doubler #52 (cont'd)

2. Ask yourself what specific or overall point the speaker seems to be making. Try to rephrase it in your own terms. (For example, the speaker might be saying, "*The Making of a Newspaper* is a new half-hour videotape showing how a newspaper brings its readers news and information every day. Learn how a newsroom operates, how stories are selected, how columnists decide on what they'll write, how stories, pictures, and advertising are put in, how the paper is printed, and how it is distributed to readers. This video is great for schools, potential advertisers, those interested in pursuing a career with a newspaper, or even for those writing or taping stories about them." You might restate it to yourself as, "This is about a video that shows everything about how a newspaper is made, from the stories to the printing. It would be great for anyone who needs to know or even is just curious about newspapers.")

3. Listen with your feelings. Let them point the way toward things your mind missed. (When what a speaker says gives you a noticeable feeling of "wrongness" or "rightness"—or any other feeling—without your having noticed anything in the speaker's words, review the last minute or two carefully. It's likely you will discover something critical you consciously missed when it went by the first time.)

4. Keep asking yourself if you understand what is being said. (It's easy to become confused when a speaker begins talking about "metacognition," and what you don't understand you can't recall clearly. But when you ask for clarification and learn, for instance, it's just a fancy word for "thinking about thinking," it's easy to follow what's being said.)

5. Listen for something you can offer an intelligent comment on. Or ask a question, point out an error, recount an illuminating anecdote. (Say an expert mentions the necessity for remembering that the largest office towers or the smallest home is a habitation for people and that architects should never forget common human needs when designing any building. You may not have much knowledge of architecture, but the statement sparks your memory of a foolish incident you read about in the local paper while in Sacramento, California. It seems the architect who designed the new library forgot to include any restrooms in his plans; he didn't do much reading, and it never occurred to him that anyone would stay at a library long enough to need such facilities. You share this anecdote with the speaker and the audience. Everyone laughs. The speaker states that was exactly the point and adds another example equally blatant.)

6. Ignore distractions. If you are easily distracted, it may take a while to get the hang of this. Implementing all the preceding strategies will help

BRAIN POWER DOUBLER #52 (cont'd)

you concentrate more closely on what is being said, despite distraction. The rest is just training your attention. Anytime you catch yourself being distracted by something that draws your attention away from the speaker's words, make a conscious effort to bore back mentally on the words. Keep doing this often enough and you'll soon get in the habit of keeping your attention centered on the speaker, no matter how he or she might act or what goes on around you.)

Chapter 12

LISTENING ONE-ON-ONE

More than 50 percent of the information we get comes one-on-one. It occurs in direct interactions between us and another person (or persons)—a co-worker dropping in to review a mutual task; the supervisor summoning everyone for a pep talk; the VP from the home office explaining the way the new bimonthly payroll system will work; a lecturer asking for questions; even your mother detailing an important family genealogy. Sometimes being a good listener isn't enough. That's because listening is a two-way street. There's a second person in the equation. To a large degree, the quality of the speaker determines the quality of your experience.

Take the story of Mishka. She was vice president in charge of strategic planning for a multimillion-dollar engineering firm. Everyone felt it would benefit the company to have a presence on the World Wide Web. But no one knew enough about the Web to answer the key questions involved: Should they expect it to increase revenues or serve mainly as a promotional tool? How could they design a home page that would attract the specific kinds of manufacturing firms that could use their services? How much work would be involved on their end, and who would be the best individual to oversee the page?

Fortunately, one of the top experts in how business could best profit from the Web was about to hold a one-day seminar in their city. Mishka's firm delegated her to attend and come back with answers to all their questions.

Mishka was due, however, to have a frustrating and disappointing experience. She found the person presenting the seminar was an expert in making money from the Web, just as advertised. (He had built a shoestring company into a 40-million-dollar-a-year operation through innovative and cutting-edge use of his homesite.)

But he was also a poor presenter. The man Mishka had come to hear rambled, mumbled his words, and was clearly uncomfortable with public speaking. Even when people asked him questions directly, he never quite seemed to get his point across. Though the man might have known everything there was to know about advancing corporate interests through the Web, very little of it actually came through.

Mishka returned from the seminar deeply annoyed. She felt she had lost a rare opportunity and that the entire experience had been a waste of time. Mishka knew she would have to devote a lot of research time to finding out what the seminar presenter already knew but had been unable to express.

Let's face it. Some people are poor speakers. They either have difficulty expressing themselves or else they go to the opposite extreme and ramble on forever without reaching a point.

No matter how acute your own listening skills, it can be nearly impossible to extract anything useful from such a person. You may be applying all your brain power in listening to what he or she has to say, but the truth is the speaker isn't saying much worth listening to.

Most speakers aren't that bad, of course. The real problem speakers lie at two extremes: Those who talk too little and those who talk too much. I call them "the reluctant," "the nonspeaker," and "the rambler." You have certainly encountered them yourself many times.

❑ Reluctant speakers, for whatever reasons, are reluctant to talk or reply in more than a few monosyllables, and those words are uttered with great difficulty.

❑ Ramblers go on and on, sometimes entertainingly, without ever saying anything of substance.

Typically, like Mishka, you leave such a speaker aurally empty-handed. You feel cheated, promised far more by the experience than was delivered. And, as with Mishka, you have the frustrating certainty that there was meat in that nut, if only you had known how to crack it.

But you don't have to come away from such an encounter with nothing to show for it. These don't have to be wasted opportunities. Just as you apply leverage with a nutcracker to get the meat out of the shell, you can multiply your listening power by applying mental leverage to extract nuggets of wisdom from even the most inadequate speaker.

Psychologists have devised a kind of linguistic jujitsu designed to draw the information from even the poorest speakers. It doesn't matter where you are: a lecture, on a phone call, at an impromptu office gathering, or at a meeting of the board. When interaction is appropriate—whether it's a question-and-answer period afterward or just a general free-for-all—these potent verbal tactics will guarantee the quality of the speaker never determines again the quality of your experience.

THE FIVE SILENCE BUSTERS

Mishka's problem was the reluctant speaker. These are people of few words in the classic sense. The problem is that they use too darned few words as far as you're concerned. Inside their skulls is a gold mine of wisdom you need to extract, but it's buried beneath a mountain of silence.

Some people say too little because they are afraid of saying too much; they know their subject so well they believe everyone else knows it too and don't want to bore listeners with the details. Other speak reluctantly because they aren't certain whether what they have to say is worthwhile or will be appreciated. Some simply have few verbal skills and little background in using them well.

As far as you are concerned, it doesn't matter. Your concern isn't their psychological quirks but how to pry those all-precious verbal tidbits of knowledge out of them. Unless it's shared, reluctant speakers' expertise is no good to them or to their listeners.

"The nonspeaker," performance consultant K. Thomas Finley writes, "may have a world of wisdom to impart, but unless she can be made to speak, no one is going to get a chance to listen to her. No one is going to learn much from her."

Following are five "Silence Busters" I developed when conducting interviews for professional publications. They never fail to coax a flow of words from the most taciturn and bashful individual. The Silence Busters will more than leverage your listening power in dealing with reluctant speakers. The five Silence Busters are

❑ Draw them out with praise.

❑ Ask pointed questions.

❑ Make a comment that provokes response.

❑ Once they start talking, don't interrupt.

❑ Give positive visual feedback.

Draw Them Out With Praise, Then Ask Questions

Even the shyest person blossoms under praise. Let reluctant speakers know their efforts are appreciated or their expertise is valued. Then invite them to amplify on their remarks. Phrase your question so it implies only a person with their exceptional background and insights could answer it.

Even when someone is taciturn or parsimonious with words, positive feedback of this kind will entice him or her to unbend a bit. When it comes to listening, flattery will get you everywhere.

Ask Pointed Questions

Short-spoken people, the "yep" and "nope" type, are comfortable with as few words as possible. Work with the grain instead of against it. You can turn their verbal parsimoniousness to your advantage. Determine precisely what it is you want to know. Then ask a question so pointed it calls for a "yes or no" answer or a brief, fact-filled one that takes no more than a sentence or two.

Make a Comment That Provokes Response

Even the most reluctant fish will rise to the proper bait. To lure reluctant speakers from their silence, bait your verbal hook with a controversial statement or question. This time try to phrase what you want to know in a way that seems to challenge the speaker's position politely or that otherwise flies in the face of established theory. Few people can resist replying when a pet idea is challenged or when they are presented with the opportunity to debunk a popular misconception.

Once They Start Talking—Don't Interrupt

Once you've managed to get reluctant speakers going, keep your own mouth shut. Disrupting the flow by interjecting a comment of your own will only give them an excuse to stop, and getting them started in the first place was difficult enough. Even if you think of a vital question or a brilliant remark, don't say it. Save your remarks until you are absolutely certain the reluctant speakers have finished.

Give Positive Visual Feedback

To keep reluctant speakers talking, you need to let them know that the details are interesting, that what is being said is worthwhile, that even if they aren't the world's best speaker you are eager for them to keep going. But don't make the encouragement verbal. That will only distract them.

Use body language. Send them positive feedback through visual cues. Nod your agreement. Smile approvingly. Stare intently into the speaker's eyes as if what he or she is saying is the most interesting thing you ever heard.

Brain Power Doubler #53

Don't ever let someone's short-spokenness be a problem again. The Silence Busters strategies will draw speaker out even the most backward speaker and keep him or her talking until you've heard what you are listening for. When you need information from reluctant speakers:

1. Use praise to draw them out. Then ask a question that obviously draws on their expertise. ("I never really understood before how many different ways there were my firm could take advantage of the Web, Mr. McDougal. As an authority, could you tell us a bit more about whether we are better off buying software and designing and maintaining our own, or would we be better off to farm it out?")

2. Ask a direct question. ("Could you tell me, Mr. McDougal, just exactly how much increase in business a firm like ours might realistically expect during its first year on the Web?")

BRAIN POWER DOUBLER #53 (cont'd)

3. Make a comment or ask a question that provokes a response. ("A story I read in the *Globe* seems to contradict your position. It stated that the majority of companies who go on the Web experience no noticeable increase in business at all. How would you respond?")

4. Once they start talking, don't interrupt until they've finished.

5. Encourage them to continue talking with positive feedback—smile, nod, make eye contact.

GETTING RAMBLERS TO THE POINT

To you, the poet Samuel Taylor Coleridge is the author of "The Rime of the Ancient Mariner." To his friends, he was a pain in the you-know-where. As one writer scathingly put it, "Nearly all commentators have stressed the difference between great talkers and great conversationalists. Irrepressible talkers kill conversation and exhaust those they are with."

Coleridge was a nonstop talker, and no one else could get a word in edgewise. More than one biographer claims that Coleridge once cornered an acquaintance at their club and began to monopolize the conversation, going on at great length about his opinions and insights in the affairs of the seventeenth century. After awhile, Coleridge became so intent on what he was saying, he closed his eyes so he could concentrate better. The friend had an appointment elsewhere in London and took the opportunity to depart. Hours later, when the man returned, Coleridge was still talking, eyes closed, unaware his friend had ever left.

Pretty funny as an anecdote. We all have a friend or acquaintance like that. We probably have a story about the person just as hilarious as the one about Coleridge. But it's not so funny when you are wasting valuable time trying to get information from someone who rambles at great length but never seems to make a useful point. Then the rambler's excess verbiage becomes an obstacle between him and your goal. Worse, there's scientific evidence that ramblers are so irritating they decrease your brain power and make following their point nearly impossible, even when they do make one. "Loud, incessant chatter is a major contributor to lost productivity and impaired performance," according to summaries of one Dayton University department of psychology study. Prolonged chatter makes listeners nervous, interferes with concentration, and dulls their ability to absorb information and remember it.

Performance consultant K. Thomas Finley has, however, developed four highly effective strategies for getting your brain power back on track by turning off ramblers' spigots of words and guiding them quickly to the point:

- ❏ Ask what their point is.
- ❏ Ask what their conclusions are.
- ❏ Guess where they are heading and ask if you are right.
- ❏ Ask another member of the group to comment on it.

Ask What Their Point Is

When a speaker rambles on without ever seeming to get anywhere, interrupt them politely. (You may have to do this two or three times, but be persistent. Remember, however, to remain polite throughout—you want enlightenment, not argument.)

When you have the rambler's attention, confess you are lost and ask them if they could help straighten you out by summarizing the overall points they are making. By taking responsibility for not understanding, you avoid arousing their defenses. By asking them to help you get it straight, you enlist their efforts by giving them a chance to show off their expertise by magnanimously assisting even the dimwitted to get it right.

(If you get the really difficult speakers, the super-ramblers, they may even take off at a tangent in trying to summarize themselves. This leaves you no better off than before. When this happens, politely interrupt and start the process again.)

Ask What Their Conclusions Are

This is simply a variant of the above. Sometimes when asking speakers what their point is fails, just asking them the same thing in different terms can do the trick. Believe it or not, there are actually people for whom "point" and "conclusion" have two different meanings and they will talk forever in search of a "point" if asked for one but can tell you their "conclusions" in a moment if asked for that by name.

Guess Where They Are Heading and Ask If You Are Right

In extreme cases, some ramblers seem unable to get their point into words, no matter how much they thresh about verbally. When this happens, your only option is to do the job for them.

Take your best guess as to where these speakers might be heading and ask them if you are right. If they say "yes," you are home free. If you are wrong, in correcting you, these ramblers might make their own point. Even when ramblers do no more than indicate you are wrong and then wander off into a verbal cabbage patch again, you are a step closer to your goal. You have at least eliminated a possible point. Just keep politely but firmly repeating the whole process until something clicks.

Ask Someone Else There for Help

If all else fails, enlist audience aid. When nothing you can do seems to elicit the point, it's likely everyone else present is just as far at sea as you are. Maybe one of them can figure out what the rambler is attempting to get at.

If you know anyone present, call on him or her. As always, take the blame on your shoulders to keep from putting the speaker on the defensive. Then appeal to a friend, or anyone else there, and ask if he or she can enlighten you.

A remark like this also makes it practically impossible for the rambler to continue without seeming rude or arrogant. No reasonable person would ignore two of their listeners. Often, it is just the boost the rambler needs to finally get to the point.

BRAIN POWER DOUBLER #54

1. Politely ask the speaker what point he is trying to make. ("I may be a little dense, Mr. McDougal, but what exactly is your point in regard to the confidentiality of data sent from our website to our headquarter's computers?")

Brain Power Doubler #54 (cont'd)

2. Politely ask him what he ultimately concludes from the data he is presenting. ("Your review of growth statistics on corporate websites over the last three years is very fascinating. But I wonder if you could tell me what conclusions they have led you to.")

3. Take your own guess at where he is heading and ask if you are right. ("If I am correct, Mr. McDougal, you are saying the new encryption programs assure absolute confidentiality of all customer inquiries sent via our website to our headquarters?")

4. Appeal to someone else there for help. ("I must be having an off night, but I'm still having trouble understanding your point. Perhaps another member of the audience could help me out here.")

Chapter 13

LISTENING
"BETWEEN THE LINES"

These days being a good listener isn't enough. Being an excellent listener isn't enough. These days listeners have to hear more than just the words. They have to listen "between the lines."

Often there is as much meaning—sometimes more—in what is not said as in what is said, especially in what is deliberately left out. Discover that meaning and you more than double your listening power.

People don't just present information. Frequently they manipulate it. Even being an instant listener isn't enough. Everyone manipulates information sometimes. We favor ourselves and Aunt Sue when we describe the funny incident with the cop (that wasn't so funny then). We try to present ourselves well, usually better than we feel we are, to others.

But more and more frequently, in more and more ways, people manipulate what they say in order to manipulate you. It's a universal that spans from the boardroom to the bedroom, encompassing all points in between.

Throughout the week, we hear dozens—and for urbanites more likely hundreds and for those with cable television it is perhaps thousands—of people seeking to sway us by manipulating the words they speak.

Scientists call it "persuasive communication." They define it as "the process through which people attempt to influence the beliefs or actions of others."

Some speakers have a bigger investment in manipulating us than others. "Persuasive communication plays a central role in a number of professions," notes Robert R. Allen, professor of Communication Arts at the University of Wisconsin. "Lawyers, salespersons, advertising specialists, public relations experts, and politicians must use persuasive communication. While persuasive communication may not be the central ingredient in many careers, most people need to be able to influence others in work-related settings."

And attempt to influence us they do. Information manipulation (AKA persuasive communication) is everywhere. It might be that phone call telling you that you have won a free weekend for two in Acapulco departing from San Diego—and all you have to do is purchase a ticket to San Diego. Or it could be the presentation by your company's health-care provider extolling the advantages of a new improved schedule of services designed with your needs in mind, which actually turns out to be the same old less-choice-and-less-care-for-more-premiums ploy tricked up to seem as if they're doing you a favor. Or it could be an employer pulling a long face and spouting figures that show a downturn in profits to justify skipping the cost-of-living raise again this year. Or an employee shuffling details to cover up a major snafu. Or an activist out to sway the public into passionate support of "the cause" and the speaker's own pocketbook. Or a professor attempting to subtly undercut a rival's thesis in a slanted review. Or a politician's selecting an opponent's words and positions—or the politician's own—to create a false impression in your mind.

Of course, not everyone who seeks to sway us through words does so with willful intent. Many can be free of any conscious desire to manipulate what they say. But they may still slant it unconsciously or may misdirect listeners unintentionally.

People tend to mislead others for one of three reasons. They may have

❐ Unconsciously (and consciously) held prejudices that cause them to distort what they perceive and what they present.

❐ Hidden agendas and are bending what they say to achieve their own ends.

❐ Different meanings for critical words and terms so that, while they mean to be clear, they nevertheless seriously mislead their audiences.

Semioticians and psychologists have, however, devised a trio of highly effective strategies for instantly recognizing all three kinds of information manipulation and for sifting what such speakers have to say for any objective facts it may contain. With them, you will be able to spot hidden agendas, discover hidden meanings, and uncover hidden truths by reading the speaker's body language.

SPOTTING HIDDEN AGENDAS

The advertisement promised those with family or individual income of over $150,000 a proven, legal method of cutting their yearly federal income tax by 50 percent and more! In smaller type, it announced a $100-a-ticket lecture by Joe Dokes (not his real name), billed as one of the country's leading authorities on personal tax reduction. Joe opened the lecture with a few humorous but deadly accurate remarks about the inequities in the tax system. He moved on to recount some flagrant and tragic cases in which honest, hardworking people had been financially ruined, even jailed, through rigid interpretations of the current code. Then he cited a half dozen specific loopholes in the income tax laws most people didn't know about (if you could have made use of them all, you could save up to 50 percent on your own taxes). Joe Dokes closed by mentioning that there were only about 230 other loopholes that tax reduction attorneys and experts were aware of but that time didn't permit going into them all.

After enthusiastic applause, audience members wanted to know how they could get more information on those 230 loopholes. Joe Dokes replied with a droll remark about the best method is to "hire the world's most expensive tax attorney." When the laughter settled down, Joe explained that there was a foundation somewhere in the Midwest that served as central clearinghouse for such information. When his listeners besieged him for the foundation's address, Joe said he thought he had it somewhere, fumbled around in his briefcase, and gave it to them. Everyone left in an up mood.

So where's the stinger?

The seemingly dispassionate and disingenuous Mr. Dokes had a hidden agenda. There was some truth in what he said about the loopholes, though the matter was not as simple or as cut and dried as he made it seem. But Mr. Dokes also had a hidden agenda that shaped every word he had spoken, from stirring up the audience's anger toward the tax system to his casual mention that there are 230 other loopholes in the code. Dokes was the owner, through a series of "fronts," of the "foundation somewhere in the Midwest that serves as a clearinghouse" for information on those loopholes. The foundation offered to sell its database to those who wrote in asking for information, and the selling price was well more than a thousand dollars.

Almost all people have some kind of hidden agenda when they speak. That's not cynicism talking. It's a fact. It's a fact of human nature. It's built into us, probably hardwired into us. And quite often hidden agendas are benign.

Think over the last day. While you were being polite to Denise from the purchasing office, were you really trying to get it over with as quickly as possible so you could get back to a rush project? When you took the job, did you tell your employers it was your hope to see them enter the twenty-first century by networking all the computers? When you told that parent about the school system's rising scores in statewide competency tests, did you fail to mention that overall violence was up and attendance was down?

Sometimes hidden agendas can be benign. But most often they are designed to mislead us so that the other person can gain an advantage over us. But you never have to worry about being manipulated by someone with a hidden agenda again. You can spot those who have them even before they open their mouths to speak (that's faster than instantly). That's because behind every hidden agenda is a hidden motive.

How can you tell a speaker's motive? Most people with hidden agendas have something to gain. You can prescreen speakers for hidden motives with this foolproof five-part test. Ask yourself if the person speaking could

❐ Gain financially by what she has to say?

❐ Gain in status?

❐ Gain in followers and publicity?

❐ Gain anything in the future?

❐ Be working off his own anger or frustration?

Once you know the answer to these questions, you should have a fairly good picture of whether you are listening to unbiased judgment or of whether the speaker is someone with a motive who is slanting her words to manipulate you to advance a hidden agenda of her own.

Brain Power Doubler #55

When anyone talks, mentally review the following five questions. They'll act like radar, zeroing in on concealed bias. You'll never again need to fear being manipulated or exploited by misrepresented information.

1. Does the person talking have anything to gain financially or otherwise by what he has to say? (Does he have books, a seminar, or a product to sell?)

2. Will the speaker gain status by having her views accepted? (It could be academic status, professional status, community status, or any other form of "standing" in others' eyes.)

3. Could he be seeking followers and/or fame? (Does he have a movement whose numbers could grow? Is there adulation or publicity involved?)

4. Can the speaker gain some future advantage with her current words? (A promotion? More customers? Nomination to office when the next election comes around?)

5. Is the speaker using words to rid himself of frustrations? (Anger at an "unfair" situation?)

DISCOVERING WHAT SPEAKERS HIDE

Everyone in the company was assembled in the cafeteria. They were to hear a presentation from Rosebud, Inc., a new HMO, bidding for the company's business. The contract with the company's old HMO had lapsed, and several health-care providers were vying for the account.

"As you probably know," the woman from Rosebud began, "we have one of the highest ratings for member satisfaction in the health-care industry. Surveys show those who use Rosebud-approved clinics give it top marks in five out of five categories of care."

She smiled to telegraph the joke she was about to make. "To be fair about it, nobody's really complaining about the care they receive in the other top HMOs either."

She waited for the laughter to subside. "I'd like to give you an item-by-item comparison of how their services compared to ours, but I can't because they could sue. . . ."

If there's ever a time when people don't say what they mean, it's when they are trying to sell you something, convince you of something, or get you to agree to something. These are times when all speakers cover up what they are really thinking, any weaknesses in their argument, and any inconvenient facts that might contradict it. Obviously, if you found out everything they knew, you might draw a different picture and reach a different conclusion from the one they intend for you to have.

Fortunately, even as speakers attempt to hide information they don't want you to become aware of, they unwittingly give away its presence by the use of certain "flag words." Whenever you hear any of these words, go on the alert and begin to listen "between the lines." Flag words are a dead giveaway that there are serious flaws in what is being said and that something is being kept from you.

A sample of some of the "flag words" you are most likely to hear follows. Flag words take many forms, and there are many more variations than can be listed in this book. But you can always recognize flag words and phrases—whatever form they take—because they all have one thing in common: Flag words contain no actual information themselves.

Instead, flag words imply something about the quality of that information. Typically, they suggest that what is being said is genuine or that there is no real contradiction or that there is no possible way the speaker can make a better offer. Intensify your listening power and suspect hidden information when you hear

❒ Words that imply a high degree of certainty.

❒ Words that minimize the downside.

❒ Words meant to tell you the other person can't compromise.

Review the anecdote about the Rosebud HMO. Can you spot the flag words and phrases in it? If not, you'll have no trouble after finishing this section. Review it, and when you find the flag words, ask yourself what the speaker might be concealing. You'll be well prepared for detecting hidden information when you encounter it in the future.

Words That Imply a High Degree of Certainty

Keep an ear out for phrases that seek to convince you there is no possible doubt about the facts or conclusion. These are usually inserted before a statement to give an apparent boost to its credibility. Beware anytime you hear phrases such as: "As you probably know. . . ,"

"Naturally . . . ," "Of course . . . ," "Everyone . . . ," "No doubt . . . ," "One thing you can always count on. . . ." These kinds of phrases are a sure tip-off that what follows isn't nearly as written in concrete as the person speaking wants you to think.

Words That Minimize the Downside

Beware phrases deliberately designed to minimize what follows. The speaker wants to make the point or data seem unimportant so you will overlook it. But the opposite is true—it is very important and conceals a hidden downside or unpleasant fact. You'll usually find them at either the start or the middle of sentences. They include "Incidentally . . . ," "I should probably . . . ," "By the way . . . ," "In passing . . . ," "To be fair about it . . . ," "Since we are speaking of. . . ." When you hear these, be alert—important information that seriously compromises what the speaker is saying is about to come up.

Words Meant to Suggest the Other Person Can't Compromise

Listen for statements that suggest it's impossible for the other person to give you what you want. When someone goes to a lot of trouble to explain to you why he or she can't make concessions, it's usually the other way around. The issue at stake is more than likely one the person can afford to meet you halfway over. Sure tip-offs are "I can't because . . . ," "Unfortunately . . . ," "My hands are tied . . . ," "It's company policy. . . ." They and their ilk are all red flags signaling you that the other person could do precisely what you want, but is hoping to prevent you from insisting on it.

BRAIN POWER DOUBLER #56

No matter who is speaking or what the situation, be alert for any of these phrases, or their cousins. When you hear them, pay attention. The other person is slanting what he or she says to advance a hidden agenda.

1. Listen for words that imply a high degree of certainty. A snow job is coming on. ("As you probably know, the investment opportunities in Belize are really fabulous." "Of course, that's the most we can possibly offer for the job." "Naturally, everyone is upset by the government's actions.")

BRAIN POWER DOUBLER #56 (cont'd)

2. Listen for words that minimize the downside. The person is trying to sweep something important under the verbal rug. ("Incidentally, there is a little problem with the roof." "I should probably mention that not everyone who goes into the commodities market prospers." "By the way, there have been some complaints about the cafeteria food.")

3. Listen for words meant to suggest the other person can't compromise. These are blatant giveaways the person will do exactly what you want, if you just ask. "Unfortunately, the high tax base prevents me from lowering the rent." "I can't deliver the bound magazines in 30 days without adding a rush charge because I would have to keep one crew working overtime." "I'd like to sell you the car for that price, but my hands are tied; it's dealership policy.")

REVEALING HIDDEN TRUTHS WITH BODY LANGUAGE

Vladamar was vice-president of his father's small trucking company. He had some money to invest. Vladamar went to a broker that a friend recommended. The broker recommended a computer manufacturer that had undergone a period of declining market share but was now under a new CEO famed for turning corporate bottom lines around.

Vladamar was curious about the forthcoming product line, which was rumored to be problem-plagued. The broker settled back, crossed his arms, and explained that a new tech team brought in by the new CEO had done a crash redesign to eliminate the last remaining bugs. Vladamar asked whether the company's liquidity and line of credit were sufficient to carry it through the promotion and launching of the line and to fund increased manufacturing if it proved a hit. The broker looked out the window for a moment, then told Vladamar a consortium of international banking firms had agreed to back an increased line of credit.

Vladamar had a last query. He had heard that the broker's firm was pushing the computer company's stock very strongly. The broker crossed his legs. The firm was merely convinced that this was the overlooked growth stock of the next 18 months, he answered.

Vladamar told the broker he would think about it. Then he went out and got a different broker and invested in a different company. He knew the first broker was bogus and so was every word he said about the computer firm.

Why? What did Vladamar catch that you missed? (Read the rest of this section and when you finish the exercise at the end, reread the preceding paragraphs and you'll pick up on everything Vladamar noticed.)

You've heard that seeing is believing? When it comes to listening, seeing can tell you what to believe too. You can multiply your listening power and tell true from false when you know the visual clues to look for.

When people are lying or being defensive or have an emotional stake in what they are saying, their body language gives them away, writes psychologist Lawrence Sloman, Ph.D. These speakers may think they are concealing their true thoughts. But, Dr. Sloman says, someone who knows the signs can see through the deception from the start. Every movement deceivers make, including many they are unaware of, tells someone who knows what to look for that the full truth is not being disclosed.

In a study published in *The American Journal of Psychiatry,* Dr. Sloman found that three simple physical movements reveal the hidden truth of what a speaker is saying. No matter how well constructed the speaker's words, his or her body language clearly reveals there is more concealed in the words than meets the ears. Examine carefully "between the lines" when someone suddenly

- ❑ Looks away.
- ❑ Shifts position.
- ❑ Crosses his or her arms.

Look Away

It turns out there is some truth to the old adage about the shifty-eyed villain. Be on guard when speakers look away from the people they are talking to, especially up at the ceiling or down at the floor. It's almost a certainty that what they are about to say is a lie.

Shift Position

Take note when people speaking suddenly cross their legs in a chair or shift position on a podium. Changes in position are a signal the subjects they are talking about are emotionally charged. Bias of some kind is likely. Try to guess what they feel about it and how this might be coloring what you hear.

Cross Their Arms

Take warning when persons talking cross their arms. The topic at hand is making them defensive. It's a sign their argument is weak or that they have something to conceal.

Brain Power Doubler #57

The following three warning signs will tell you what someone is saying might be deceptive or be a weak spot in their argument or be the result of emotional bias. During verbal presentations, watch for

1. Places where the speaker suddenly looks away. (If it's rosy corporate prospects for next year, or how the lamp came to be broken, or how big that fish he caught in 1985 was, chances are you're not listening to the full truth about the matter.)

2. Places where they suddenly shift position. (From oil production to fiber-optic cable to those miscreants in office, it's a good bet she has strong feelings about the topic.)

3. Places where they cross their arms. (When mentioning a contrary opinion, when asked a question by someone else, they are seriously defensive about something.)

DOUBLING YOUR
THINKING POWER

natural thinking power. When you have heightened and honed your ability to think, you can truly feel that you are using all of your mind all of the time.

This chapter is a refresher course designed to make you more adept at tapping into your own natural thinking power and to help get your own mental processes going instantly any time they become stuck. The next chapter will show you how to hone those powers and apply them successfully to problems, challenges, and situations that would have daunted you alone. The final chapter contains strategies for putting what you think into action.

JUMP-START YOUR THINKING PROCESSES

Sometimes you find yourself in the situation of having your mind all pumped up with information, but you aren't going anyplace mentally. The fuel is in the tank, the key is in the lock and has been turned, but your mental engine isn't turning over. Some vital connection necessary to get the spark of thought lit isn't being made.

When you are in an important meeting or working on a vital project under an urgent deadline, drawing a mental blank rather than generating a productive train of thought can leave you feeling frustrated and embarrassed. But you don't have to sit there like a dunce anymore.

Just as you can bridge the missing electrical connection and fire up your engine by hot-wiring your car, so can you supply the missing mental connection and start your mind turning over by jump-starting your thinking processes. You're about to discover five mental jumping-off points guaranteed to boost brain power by setting your thoughts flowing. Each will hot-wire your mind no matter how blank it is or how uninspired it feels.

- ❏ Eliminate mental static.
- ❏ Focus on the subject.
- ❏ Ask yourself what it makes you feel.
- ❏ Ask yourself what it makes you think.
- ❏ Think about everything—all the time.

Eliminate Mental Static

The biggest obstacle to getting started thinking is—thinking. Usually our minds are filled with a thousand flitting thoughts. They act like mental static, making it hard for us to focus in clearly on what we want to be thinking about. Reduce this mental chatter and your thinking power will increase exponentially.

Focus on Thinking About Your Subject

You can order your mind to focus its attention. The commands take a few minutes before they begin to work. But making a deliberate effort to impress on your mind the fact that you want to think about U.S. Forestry Department statistics or how to word process with Wordmaker 2001 will soon get your brain up and running and generating ideas on that topic.

Ask What It Makes You Feel

If you have trouble getting started thinking, get started feeling. People often draw a mental blank when they have to sit down and do formal, "serious" thinking. If you can't get in touch with your thoughts, get in touch with your feelings. Asking yourself what you feel about it—even if it's boredom—will get your inner mental dialogue going.

Ask What It Makes You Think

When you desperately need two thoughts to rub together and nothing comes, step back a bit—don't think about the subject you are supposed to be thinking about. Try some "metacognition": Ask yourself instead what you think about the subject. This amazing technique has often served to launch a long and successful train of thought.

Think About Everything—All the Time

It's easier to get a car engine going when it's still warm. It's easier to get your thought processes working if you get your mind accustomed to thinking frequently. Thinking is a habit, and one you can get into. Evaluate, question, compare, and otherwise think about everything that goes on around you, all the time. Besides, as research by psychologist Eric Klinger demonstrates, stray thoughts often lead to solutions for perplexing problems.

Brain Power Doubler #58

Use this technique in any circumstance in which you need brain power, but just can't seem to get your mind to work.

1. Take five minutes to breathe slowly and clear your mind of extraneous mental static.

2. Deliberately, consciously, and with as much will as you can muster, order your mind to focus on and think about your subject. Then actively begin thinking about it yourself. (You may still encounter difficulty getting started, but even thinking about it a little bit or thinking the most elementary thoughts will help prime the pump. Soon you will find your mind is up and running along automatically thinking smoothly without your having to consciously will it on.

3. Ask yourself what you feel about the subject. Be honest. Tune in on yourself. When you have the answer, ask yourself why you feel that way. (There! You are already thinking about the subject. Now wasn't that easy?)

4. Ask yourself what you think about the subject. You may not know how to start thinking about it, but you do know what you think. (What is your overall evaluation of the subject? What do you consider the key points? What causes you the most concern?)

5. Use your mind all the time. Think about everything—not just what you have to. Ask yourself questions about what causes things, why people act the way they do, compare what's happening to something similar that happened some time ago, decide what you think about what you see on television. Keep your thinking processes shaken up and going throughout each day. That way your mind won't need to be jump-started—it will always be "up and running."

NEVER-FAIL BRAIN STARTERS

If all else fails, if your mind remains stubbornly resistant, if you just can't seem to find a suitable place to launch your thinking from, if you can't seem to get a coherent line of thought going—don't give up the ship! Motivation experts like Michael McCarthy have stepped in to help by developing brain-teasing questions that apply to almost any situation. The four Brain Starters below are so profound and so provocative that they will get even the blankest, most sluggish mind off and running.

❏ What is the linchpin idea?

❏ Does anything remind you of something you have experienced or seem parallel to something you already know?

❏ Is there any fact or statement you have a nagging question about?

❏ What is the bottom line?

BRAIN POWER DOUBLER #59

Use the four Brain Starters to generate thinking power to spare, and no matter how new, difficult, or boring the matter at hand, you'll never be mentally stumped for a place to begin. By the time you finish, you'll discover your mind is racing along, actually enjoying thinking about the subject.

1. Focus on the situation, information, or problem that you can't seem to start thinking about.

2. Say to yourself: "What seems to me the key, most important, or linchpin idea here?" Then take the time to really think about the answer.

3. Say to yourself: "Does this remind me of or parallel anything I have already learned or experienced?" Again, take time to really find and ponder an answer.

4. Say to yourself: "Is there anything I still have a nagging question about?" Once more, take the time to think about and answer the question.

5. Say to yourself: "When I put it all together, what do I think is the bottom line?" Again, consider an answer carefully.

ONE STEP TO CRYSTAL-CLEAR THOUGHT

To whom hasn't this happened? You have a brilliant series of inspirations: a far more efficient way of structuring your franchising operations; a can't-lose sales promotion; a proposal for the hospital board of directors for a vitally needed item of equipment.

But when you sit down to write it or stand up in committee to make your pitch, you can't quite put the idea across in words. Things are clear in your thoughts, but they get all tangled up or lack power or clarity.

After all, what good are our most brilliant thoughts if we can't express them clearly to others? For that matter, what good are they to us if we can't express them clearly to ourselves?

The situation gets even worse when statistics and other "dry" facts are involved. Even the most accomplished presenters and writers experience difficulty communicating them clearly and understandably. Most of the rest of us just flounder around.

People who choose to write serious, technically accurate science fiction have it even harder. They must show abstract, technical, and often highly complicated material in a form that is understandable to the general reading public. It's a challenge, and one my friend, award-winning author Larry Niven, found his own unique way to solve.

Before he would write a story, he would tell it to friends at cocktail parties. If he could hold their interest and get the technical details across, he knew he had a story that was ready for writing. If their eyes glazed or their attention wandered, Niven knew he still needed to express his thoughts more clearly.

Another person who espoused this approach was publisher Jeremy Tarcher. His firm specialized in popular books on science and psychology by leading academic authorities. He advised his authors to set their thoughts down exactly as they would explain them to an interested but uninformed person they might meet at a social gathering.

This technique might sound trivial, but don't mistake its ability to clarify thinking power. When you can formulate your thoughts so clearly that other people can understand them too, you "own" the subject and can be said to have mastered it. It worked wonders for Niven, it worked for Tarcher (producing numerous best-selling and award-winning books), and it can work wonders for you.

A second advantage of this system is that you get informal feedback beforehand. People will tell you which parts of your thinking they find stimulating and which seem vague, confusing, or fallacious. By the time you are ready to set your ideas down in print or are called before that committee, you'll have had a chance to improve your presentation so that everyone present follows it clearly and considers it well thought out.

If you are acquiring information or thinking seriously about a topic over a period of time, you would do well to describe what you are learning to friends now and then as you go along. That way if you suddenly find yourself pressed to articulate what you know of it—anywhere during the process or at the end—you'll be able to bring your thoughts to the tip of your tongue and talk about them fluently and lucidly.

You might be working at a car wash and studying to become a television news cameraperson at night. You get together every week or so to play Dungeons and Dragons with a mixed group of friends. Hit them with the highlights of what you've learned—and thought about what you've learned—about the profession since you last met. Partway through the course, you might get a shot at a job operating the camera with a very small cable company and because you talk knowledgeably and cogently, are offered the position. At the least, you'll pass your exams in a whiz at the end of the course and do well on all future job interviews.

Or you might get stuck with a week to do a report on a new development in oil geology to prepare for a meeting with a manufacturing group. Bounce your thoughts on what you are discovering off colleagues, superiors, old friends, and family. If necessary, talk to yourself as you drive to and from work. When you sit down at your computer to begin the report, you won't have any trouble setting down your thoughts in words.

BRAIN POWER DOUBLER #60

Always run significant thoughts by others. This will help clarify them and reveal any unsound reasoning.

1. Next time you need to gather your thoughts on a subject for later use or presentation, begin by discussing them with a friend, colleague, or family member.

2. Listen for feedback. If you don't get any, ask for some. Ask what the others thought about what you said, what they found confusing or didn't understand, what they found interesting and why.

BRAIN POWER DOUBLER #60 (cont'd)

3. Act on the feedback. If there was a fallacy in your logic, remedy it. If you need to rethink how to describe certain details so they will come across more clearly, do so. If the other people were restless or bored, look for ways to jazz up your presentation with a funny story or a dramatic anecdote.

4. Try it again on someone else, this time with your alterations included. Does it go better? If so, you are on the right track.

Chapter 15

THREE STEPS TO POWER THINKING

Hauser was the smartest of the seniors at a prestigious Boston university. His brain never ceased whirring. He investigated everything. He asked himself questions about everything. He had thoughts about every subject, especially psychology, his major.

Hauser drove all his dorm mates buggy by peppering them with his newest insights into the human mind. He detailed the thousand and one other thoughts on psychology he planned to put in his final paper. This mental flow of ideas on the subject never seemed to abate.

But when the list of graduates was issued at the end of the year, Hauser's name wasn't among them. His professors considered his finals substandard. Hauser had done a lot of thinking about psychology, all right. But it had all been vague, poorly reasoned, inadequately researched, faulty, and illogical. Hauser's problem with thinking wasn't getting started or having something to think about, it was with the quality of his thinking.

On the other hand, Mr. Mathes had the Midas touch. He'd taken over his father's run-down television station, made the right moves at the beginning of the home cable boom, got his station on several, become a "superstation," and borrowed on that success to buy a small failing movie studio. With the inventory of old films made by the studio, he launched his own television cable movie network showing old classics; with the studio, he began making original programming for both his superstation and his cable channel. With the proceeds from those ventures, he started an all-sports network overnight that rode the Los Angeles Olympics to number one in the ratings.

An interviewer once asked Mr. Mathes his secret. How had he known to make just the right moves at just the right moment? How

185

had he known that the millions involved in purchasing the studio could be earned back through a cable channel? Or that America's sports fever over the Olympics would translate into high enough ratings to justify the millions in start-up costs?

It wasn't any special talent, Mathes said. The kind of power thinking that had turned him into a multimillionaire was an ordinary ability shared by everyone. He'd just looked each situation over, done a little simple, common-sense thinking, and come up with the right answer.

The difference between Hauser and Mathes, between humiliating failure and spectacular achievement, was nothing more complicated than simple, common-sense thinking. Put that way, it doesn't sound so hard, does it?

Most people may not think they are great "brains," but they do feel they possess a modicum of common sense and are capable of simple thinking. Chances are you probably feel the same way about yourself.

It's a little-appreciated fact, but most of the world's legendary successes—Henry Ford, Margaret Sanger, Donald Trump—are no smarter than anyone else. We assume creative people must have enormous IQs. But after numerous studies of highly successful people in all walks of life, psychologist and researcher Dean Simonton, Ph.D., found no relationship between intelligence and achievement.

What separated those who succeeded from those who failed over and over again was—as with Mr. Mathes—their ability to engage in simple, common-sense thinking. It doesn't sound difficult, does it?

Is there a trick? No! Is there a catch? No!

Since you already possess some common sense and are capable of simple thinking, you already possess the important constituents of success. You spend all day using these abilities without, well, giving it a thought.

Yet when we find ourselves in any situation that calls for "structured" thinking—a quiz we have to take, a critical analysis we are assigned to write, a presentation before important clients—we panic and find ourselves at a loss. Suddenly, we become frightened that the quality of our thought is substandard. We feel anxious, inadequate, certain we will make the wrong choice, certain we are taking too long, certain we are unusually slow, certain there are others who are better thinkers and could make a better decision. No wonder we go mentally blank, our minds empty, our thoughts becoming jumbled and vague.

The problem isn't with your ability to think. You do that all the time. The problem is that, as is the case with the other brain-power skills, you were never taught to think. Not during school and not afterward.

Mentally review your school and college days. Did you ever hear of a course called "Thinking 101" or even "How to Think for Beginners"? Actually when you stop to consider it, it's amazing that for all the hundreds of hours of information drilled into our minds between first grade and the day we graduate from a university, not one minute is devoted to teaching us how to think.

The closest it comes is a vague introduction to Aristotle's basic principles of logic sometime in high school: that a thing is itself, that it cannot simultaneously be itself and something else, and that it must be either itself or something else.

We are left to make what use we can of this and to learn to think helter-skelter on our own. What's astonishing is that we do so well at it on the whole or we wouldn't be able to hold jobs, make reasonably wise choices, or understand the majority of what is going on around us.

What we more or less think of as "structured" or "serious" thinking—problem solving, analyzing information, drawing conclusions—is nothing more than common sense applied in an orderly, systematic fashion. You can learn to do this virtually instantly, once you become adept at a few simple mental tricks. In fact, you will have become a better thinker by the time you finish the first of the three sections that follow.

Clear, common-sense thinking, the kind you do every day, often without realizing it, comes in three different forms:

❐ Logical thinking—putting two and two together to make four

❐ Inductive thinking—drawing a general conclusion after noticing a series of related facts

❐ Deductive thinking—drawing a conclusion from a valid premise

All you need to do is learn how and when to apply them and in what order.

THINKING LOGICALLY

Logical thinking sounds as if it is difficult, cumbersome, like something out of Aristotle and the Greeks. Logical thinking sounds as if it involves academic intensity, mental cogitation, mathematics and quantum physics, and all that other ultra-heavy stuff that takes a lot of effort and requires native talent. Actually it's so simple children do it.

As with the rest of "structured" thinking, it's a mental process you engage in many times each day. Logical thinking is nothing more complicated or intimidating than the process of asking yourself questions about things and trying to come up with a reasonable answer to them.

What's the definition of a "reasonable" answer? You already know that intuitively. It's something you decide for yourself every waking minute of your life. If you stop to think about it, the elements probably encompass whether the answer fits the facts and whether it is within the realm of what you consider possible.

So that's what makes it "reasonable" or "logical," you say. But how does the "thinking" part work? That's easy too; it's another of those abilities nature has already hardwired in your brain.

The "thinking" part lies in "associating" or "comparing" facts, objects, people, characteristics, and anything else our minds can encompass. You mentally gather some facts, or you might have them on hand in your mental data bank. You pick up one of those facts mentally, ask yourself a few questions about it. Then you look around in the outside world or within yourself for other facts that might relate to it. You ask yourself questions about those facts, and compare and contrast them with the first fact. If they seem to fit, you keep them; if not, you discard them.

Now where's the difficulty in that? It's something you can't help doing. Your brain is designed to tick along doing it literally every second of your life in response to everything you see, think, feel, hear, or taste. This process is so ubiquitous and constant that you probably take it for granted and never know you are doing it at all. You compare the service at different ice-cream emporiums; you compare the work habits of two employees; you compare job prospects; you compare the new movie with your favorite star to her last film; you compare the driving habits of those around you on the drive home.

But that isn't all there is to logical thinking, you protest. There's still a hard part—making judgments, reaching conclusions. That's the stuff that separates the mental pros from the amateurs; they are good at drawing conclusions and making decisions. And what led you to that conclusion? How did you reach that judgment?

So what do you think about your spouse's mother, about the deal you got on your house, about that new person who just joined your department, about whether the Democrats or the Republicans have the right idea on welfare? How did you make those judgments—how did you reach those judgments?

Face it, you are already a master of every key phase of logical thinking. And you are so good at it, you do it so naturally, so effortlessly most of the time that you never paused to analyze what you were doing or how you were doing it.

Here's a typical example: You drive past a prosperous looking lunch stand on what seems a quiet, tree-lined street. You ask yourself from where it could draw its customers. You turn the corner and discover a brand-new office park. Bingo! You have gathered an important new fact and associated that with the lunch stand. When you compare them, the two facts seem to make a perfect fit, and you conclude that the stand's prosperity is due to traffic from those who work in the office park.

The only difference with a structured learning situation—such as a division meeting, analyzing the annual corporate report of a restaurant chain in which you are heavily invested, writing a master's thesis, or figuring out how to apply a new spreadsheet program—is that you have never consciously identified these steps. Nor have you recognized your own intuitive mastery of them.

So you become flustered and consider yourself thickheaded; you panic, and since you don't have any idea where to begin or that it's something you can easily do, you feel defeated and give up before you start. Or you sweat through the process, convinced all along that your mental efforts are substandard and that everyone around you realizes what a mental dunce you are.

But you can turn this situation around and consciously become the powerful and logical thinker you already are instinctively, by remaining calm and drawing on your mind's natural abilities to

❏ Ask yourself questions.

❑ Gather associated facts.

❑ Compare them for commonalities and contrasts.

❑ Let the facts decide for you.

The next exercise will show you how to hone your own logical thinking skills and put them in action.

BRAIN POWER DOUBLER #61

You'll never again need to fear challenges to your reasoning power in school, business, or your personal life. Just remember the following four steps.

1. Ask yourself questions. (Example: A seminar leader challenges you to go home overnight, examine the facts about two comparable mutual funds, and report to him the next morning which of the two you would invest your client's money with.)

2. Gather associated facts. (You pore over the figures in the two prospectuses, their corporate figures, their past performance.)

3. Compare them for commonalities and contrasts. (You compare management, liquidity, areas of specialization, earnings.)

4. Reach a conclusion. (One of the funds has been paying higher dividends, but it has also dabbled in more volatile high-tech stocks whose earnings were subject to consumer fads. The other has more of its assets in institutional corporations supplying long-term steady demands such as food processing and automobiles. The facts have made your decision for you. You recommend the latter fund.)

THINKING INDUCTIVELY

You think inductively all the time. When you observe several facts, items, or situations (you notice that people over six feet tall have to duck when they enter the door of a certain clothing boutique) and then make a general assumption based on them (the tall woman you see approaching the store will have to duck when she enters), that's inductive thinking.

Or take another example; A businesswoman may test market a new all-natural insecticide. She test markets it using three different marketing campaigns in three different regions. One bases its pitch on the fact that it is an all-natural pest killer that is environmentally friendly. The second bases its appeal on the spray's strength, quickness, and effectiveness. The third focuses on price comparison. Her assumption is that consumers responded best to the advertisements touting strength, and she plans her national campaign accordingly.

First, she establishes the facts through experimentation and observation. Then she makes her inductive assumption: that when it came to insecticides, people are more interested in effectiveness than in anything else.

There's one drawback with inductive thinking. If the observations or facts are wrong or incomplete, the assumption will be wrong. What if a disproportionate sampling of consumer reaction to the woman's insecticide advertising was in the South, an area notorious for the hardiness of its insect population? Perhaps those in the North might have responded better to an advertising campaign emphasizing savings and the insecticide's lower price.

Assumptions arrived at through inductive thinking must always be tested in order to be certain they are correct and must be held open for revision if contradictory facts are discovered. The woman could further test market her insecticide, or she could go slow at first with the campaign heralding its potency until results convinced her that her assumption was correct.

This form of inductive thinking involves observing facts or gathering data, then reaching and testing a conclusion predicated on it. There are three steps involved:

❐ Observation

❐ Making assumptions

❐ Checking assumptions

Observing facts and asking and checking assumptions is so much a part of everyday life that you do it unknowingly throughout the day. It's inductive thinking when you assume the ice cream will taste delicious, and it does. Or when you boot up the computer and assume it will come on, and it does. You do it when you turn the key confidently in the car engine and expect it to start up, and it doesn't. Your assumption tested wrong in that case.

BRAIN POWER DOUBLER #62

You won't need to feel flustered the next time you face a challenging situation that requires you to do inductive thinking. Whether it's a report on why so many traffic accidents occur near a local school, trying to put together the pieces of a competitor's strategy, the exact reason for a bottleneck between sales and shipping, you can proceed with confidence by following these three steps.

1. Observe the facts. This could involve anything from reading to field research—whatever it takes to gather enough data.

2. Look it over to see if any general relations or patterns seem to emerge. Ask yourself what assumptions you might be able to make based on these patterns.

3. On the checking of assumptions, when possible or in doubt test all conclusions you reach via inductive thinking. Verify facts and put your conclusion into practice in a small way at first—again, do whatever you can to ensure that your assumptions do not lead you astray.

THINKING DEDUCTIVELY

"It's elementary, my dear Watson!" Sherlock Holmes, the world-celebrated fictional detective would cry to his companion. Holmes's success in his stories is due entirely to his expertise at deduction. Let him see a number of clues and he could deduce the identity of the killer.

One of his most famous deductions, he told Watson, involved the case of the dog's barking on the night of a great theft. "But the dog didn't bark during the night," Watson protested. "Precisely!" exclaimed Holmes. His deduction: that the dog must have known the thief.

Sherlock Holmes's facility at deductive thinking is nothing astounding. Deductive thinking is another innate thinking ability we were all born with. Holmes merely made the effort to use it more frequently than most of the rest normally do.

When you decide the bank you work for should be more stringent in credit requirements for video-rental stores because of their high failure and bankruptcy rate, you are thinking deductively. You are using a general principle or a collection of specific data to draw—deduce—a specific conclusion.

Deductive thinking is the opposite of inductive thinking. Instead of gathering data and then drawing a generalization, deductive thinking starts at the other end. You begin with a generalization that you think might be true, for example, that a certain company makes good software, based on having bought a number of their programs. Then you apply this generalization to a specific case and decide that their newest program should also be a winner.

You probably aren't conscious of it—the fact that we are largely unconscious of our thinking processes is a major handicap to capitalizing on them—but hidden in this simple deduction are three essential principles. These principles represent basic steps in the reasoning process. They are:

- ❏ A major premise or generalization
- ❏ A minor premise or generalization
- ❏ A conclusion or deduction

Deduction is a lot like "one plus one equals two." Considering the major premise and minor premise together usually suggests the conclusion.

In your deduction that the new software would be a good product, these principles were: major premise or generalization—the firm has always designed good programs in the past; minor premise or conclusion—the firm has a new product; deduction—the new software should be of comparable quality.

Deductive thinking shares the same drawback as does inductive thinking. It works well if your premises are accurate. If they aren't, your conclusion will be faulty. For instance, the software company might be experiencing cash-flow problems and have issued the new program before all the bugs could be removed. Or their record might not be as good as you think; they might also have produced several trouble-prone programs and you just didn't happen to purchase any of them. In either case, their new software might not prove the programming wonder you expect.

As with inductive thinking, all conclusions reached via deductive thinking need to be tested, double-checked, and otherwise subjected to proof.

BRAIN POWER DOUBLER #63

Use the exercise that follows as a model whenever you are in a situation in which you are applying general knowledge to specific cases.

1. Ask yourself what your major underlying premise or generalization is. (Holmes's generalization was that most dogs bark at strangers.)

2. Ask yourself what your minor premise is. (For Holmes it was that dogs do not bark at their owners.)

3. Add them together mentally—compare them, contrast them, see if they suggest anything to you at all. (Holmes added it all together and deduced that the thief must be one of the dog's owners.)

4. Check and double-check your major premises and be certain your logic is sound. Avoid logical fallacies such as inadequate sampling, *post hoc, ergo propter hoc* logic, or false analogy. (Holmes determined that the dog did bark at strangers and then gathered additional evidence before identifying the thief to the local police.)

Chapter 16

APPLYING
WHAT YOU THINK

Hammerfeld was the management consultant's management consultant—in one sense. He had degrees from Harvard, Berkeley, and at least one prestigious European university. He was the most omnivorous reader and Web-browser, up on all next year's trends and innovations in management and productivity theory and technique.

His friends were a *Who's Who* of the other top business consultants. They all vied with one another to take Hammerfeld to dinner to pick his brains for the juiciest tips and insights. World-famous motivational seminar leaders based their work—credited and uncredited—on little more than tidbits that had fallen from his lips.

So why haven't you heard of Hammerfeld? Why isn't his name emblazoned on your memory the way Tony Buzan and other famous management wizards are? Why aren't his books on the bestseller lists? And why hasn't he made a whirlwind tour of your city with a lecture or seminar?

Hammerfeld had plenty of brain power when it came to knowledge; he also had a mental Achilles' heel. Hammerfeld had no idea how to put what he preached into practice. Although he could supply the information that allowed other management consultants to prosper, his own consulting company did only moderately well.

Most people have a friend who, like Hammerfeld, is widely read— a real "brain" who knows something about everything. Yet for all their learning and knowledge, they just don't seem to be able to get anywhere in life. If not outright failures, they never become the terrific successes you might assume so much knowledge and learning ought to make them.

That's not necessarily their fault. There's a big difference between acquiring knowledge and making use of it. It's a lot like storing information on your hard drive. To run it, sort it, and make it output in a form that's helpful to you, a special program, a special kind of knowledge, is necessary.

You are in the market for a condo, and you research property values, the economic future of surrounding communities, and schools, as children figure in your long-term goals. The time comes to sit down and make sense of this wealth of facts and figures. You draw a blank and don't know where to begin.

Or the second vice-president in charge of marketing calendar programs for personal computers summons you into her office. She knows that as the customer service representative in charge of inquiries and complaints from the East Coast, you have learned a great deal about customers' interests and purchasing habits. She unveils a plan to launch a new series of electronic calendars targeted to people in specific regions of the country. The company intends to test market them on the East Coast, with calendars for New England, New York, and Florida at the beginning. Your input is desired, but the whole thing is so far from your normal area of expertise and involvement, you don't know how to answer or where to begin.

Frequently, we have the information we need, but when it comes time to get our minds to work on it, we don't quite know how to begin. Most approaches to learning, memory, reading, and listening load us up with ways to absorb new ideas and data. But they typically neglect to tell us how to apply what we have learned. They assume that people will just "naturally" know how to take the next step and use the knowledge in their job, class, or life.

But the step between theory and practice, between knowledge and application, can be a big one. This chapter will introduce two proven strategies to bridge that gap. Never again will information, ideas, and insights gather dust in the storehouse of your mind.

If you are someone who likes to do things in a logical, organized way, the first of the two techniques will probably work best for you. If a more free-form kind of approach is more suited to your personal style, you may get better results from the second technique. Either way, each draws on the cutting-edge research into our thinking processes; each is sure to more than double your thinking power.

USING THE SIX MODES OF THINKING

Johanna had only one goal in life. She wanted to make her mark on the world by turning her desktop publishing enterprise into a success and then replicating it across the country via franchising.

To give herself that vital edge in expertise and knowledge, Johanna attended every workshop, seminar, and lecture series on small businesses, marketing, inventory management, and success in general she could find. She would drive half a day to hear someone who had the entrepreneurial touch of gold speak before a college or business group. She even flew from coast to coast several times a year to hear the real hotshots like Tony Roberts share pearls of wisdom at high-priced conferences and seminars.

In spite of a mounting stockpile of insider business knowledge, however, Johanna's desktop publishing service remained nothing more than a successful local enterprise. People weren't standing 12 deep around the order desk, and money wasn't flowing into her coffers like wine. In fact, it didn't look very different or operate very differently from any other copying service with the newest in laser printers and computerized accessories.

Her friends were baffled. Was Johanna a dunce? Or were the nation's business wizards failing to deliver the goods for those who attended their seminars? A group of friends took her to lunch. After quizzing her closely, this is what they found: Although her head was filled with hundreds of tips, tricks, procedures, strategies, and methods, Johanna's case was similar to that of Hammerfeld's—she didn't know where to start.

Some of the ideas she had absorbed would apply to her situation; others would not. Some would work for her particular business, clientele, and locations; others could prove disastrous. Which were which? Johanna didn't know. Picking the wrong one might prove fatal. And even if she knew which was right, Johanna said she had no idea where or how to begin to implement any of the fabulous things she'd heard described.

After the lunch, one of Johanna's friends, who had attended one of my West Coast workshops, suggested she try the Six Modes of Thinking. The Six Modes of Thinking are derived from the work of

Edward de Bono, a pioneer in the teaching of thinking. They represent six completely different ways of viewing any problem or situation; added together they become a powerful tool for jump-starting your thinking processes.

The Six Modes of Thinking sextuple your brain power by having you think about the situation from each of the following viewpoints:

- ❐ Thinking objectively
- ❐ Thinking critically
- ❐ Thinking positively
- ❐ Thinking creatively
- ❐ Thinking intuitively
- ❐ Thinking about the modes

Thinking Objectively

Thinking objectively logically scrutinizes all facts, figures, and other objective information available about a situation.

Thinking Critically

Thinking critically examines a situation carefully, looking for every possible problem, downside, drawback, and negative consequence that could be associated with a situation.

Thinking Positively

Thinking positively views a situation from a positive viewpoint and searches only for possibilities, solutions, opportunities, pluses, and benefits.

Thinking Creatively

Thinking creatively projects creative solutions, combinations, and ideas that might better a situation.

Thinking Intuitively

Thinking intuitively tries to tune in with the deeper reactions to a situation, "gut feelings," the language of the heart, emotional nuances,

BRAIN POWER DOUBLER #64 (cont'd)

8. Think intuitively: Write down what you feel—good or bad or whatever it might be. (Johanna had only one more mode to try. Deep inside she felt positively about taking the step. So she did.)

9. Thinking about the modes: Back on your first page, where you defined the problem, write down what you've learned from the six modes of thinking. Which insights do you consider most valuable? What do you think your own next move should be?

USING THE NINE MAXIMS OF CREATIVE THINKING

Sometimes profound insights come to those with tidy desks, those whose files are well organized and who approach things in a logical, methodical way. But just as often inspiration strikes someone whose hair is unbrushed, who can't find that file they were looking for, and whose thinking processes are a bit more haphazard.

If you are more an intuitive, go-with-the-flow-type thinker who does best in less structured situations, try this alternate strategy for putting what you know to work. It offers a more free-form approach derived from the work of several learning and creativity researchers, especially that of Roger Schank, professor of psychology at Yale University. The following nine maxims, which differ slightly from Professor Shank's famous maxims, represent the cream of the crop of the best strategies for maximizing your thinking power.

There's nothing esoteric or difficult or even "alien" about them. Most of these maxims are "obvious"—in fact, they are all things you have done mentally at some time or another. The difference is that now you will bring them to bear consciously and in tandem whenever you are called on for creative thought.

The Nine Maxims of Creative Thinking are:

1. Get all the data—before you decide on an answer.

2. Classify—and invent new classifications.

3. Generalize, generalize.

4. Explain, explain.

5. Look for what you don't understand.

6. Apply what you've learned before.

7. Reject the standard wisdom.

8. Let your thoughts wander.

9. Give yourself permission to fail.

Get All the Data—Before You Decide on the Answer

Before you can generate a valid solution, a new approach, or a theory, drop all preconceptions and first gather all the data you possibly can. Without these data, you won't have the mental kindling to fuel your thinking process, and preconceptions can prevent us from seeing important facts or relationships.

Classify—And Invent New Classifications

Creating our own categories and classifications helps us see connections, and this leads to making generalizations.

Generalize, Generalize

Generalizations help us generate new insights, ideas, and solutions. Their importance isn't in whether we are right, but that they set us thinking.

Explain

We know something only when we understand it. And we understand it only when we can explain it to ourselves in our own terms. Trying to explain a situation or a dilemma "hot-wires" the thinking process and gets the mind started to rev up.

Look for What You Don't Understand

According to Professor Schank, understanding can arise only from not understanding. The key to thinking is what we don't understand—anomalies. Look for things that don't make sense to you, but go even farther. Pretend you don't understand anything and question everything.

Apply What You've Learned Before

Often things you already know—from entirely unrelated fields—will help spark insights and inspirations.

Reject the Standard Wisdom

Most often, the solution is staring us in the face, but we reject it because it flies in the face of the "standard wisdom" in the field. Question current explanations—they might be limiting you—because standard wisdom is so often wrong.

Let Your Thoughts Wander

Mind wandering, daydreaming, those moments when our thoughts go off at a tangent often result in fresh insights, even entire solutions. Flitting from thought to thought is still thinking, and often the unconscious is behind it, mentally adding two and two for us and pointing the direction to the answer we were seeking.

Give Yourself Permission to Fail

The path to success is littered with failure. Expect to fail, embrace it, welcome it. Consider each idea that doesn't work a step that carries you closer to the answer you seek. This gives you the freedom to take a chance since you won't hold back for fear of failing.

BRAIN POWER DOUBLER #65

The next time you need to apply what you know to a challenging situation, let the following exercise stimulate your creative thinking. The Nine Maxims will help you instantly boost your thinking power to its height when needed, whether it's for meetings, writing reports, being asked for suggestions, or when you're stuck for a method of implementing a new policy directive.

1. Get all the data before you decide on an answer. Create a file folder, gather the relevant data, and keep it there.

BRAIN POWER DOUBLER #65 (cont'd)

2. Classify—and invent new classifications. Adapt the Memory Map (Chapter 7) and use it to help you discover connections, relationships, and classifications.

3. Generalize, generalize. Write down what seem key causes, results, and categories.

4. Explain, explain. Write down explanations (in your own words) of all important principles and relationships.

5. Look for what you don't understand. List all terms, situations, results, and anything else you don't understand. Get the facts you need to understand them.

6. Apply what you've learned before. If you lack all specific knowledge of the subject—which is very rare—you will have learned many guiding principles of life, business, and human nature that are applicable to any situation.

7. Reject the standard wisdom. Just because it's never been done that way or thought of before doesn't mean it won't work. People said human beings would never fly or reach the moon. They didn't think Americans would go for raw fish wrapped in seaweed, either, but sushi restaurants dot the landscape of every major city.

8. Let your thoughts wander. Daydream a bit about the subject. Fantasize about what you want to happen and what could happen and different ways of doing this.

9. Give yourself permission to fail. This may be the most important step. Thomas Edison grew world-famous for a hundred or so inventions, including the light bulb and the record player. But he patented literally tens of thousands of inventions, most of which turned out to be completely useless. Think of each failure as a stepping stone toward success.

RECOMMENDED READING

Asimov, Isaac, *The Brain,* Houghton Mifflin, 1963.

Asimov, Isaac, *In Memory Yet Green,* Doubleday, 1979.

Benson, Herbert, M.D., *The Relaxation Response,* Morrow, 1975.

Calder, Nigel, *The Mind of Man,* Viking, 1970.

Finley, K. Thomas, *Mental Dynamics,* Prentice Hall, 1991.

Gardner, Howard, *Frames of the Mind,* Basic, 1983.

Gross, Ronald, *Peak Learning,* Tarcher, 1991.

Hampden-Turner, Charles, *Maps of the Mind,* Macmillan.

Harman, Willis, Ph.D., and Howard Rheingold, *Higher Creativity,* Tarcher, 1984.

Hooper, Judith, and Dick Teresi, *The 3-Pound Universe,* Tarcher, 1991.

Klinger, Eric, Ph.D., *Daydreaming,* Tarcher, 1990.

Lewis, David, and James Greene, *Thinking Better,* Holt, 1982.

McCarthy, Michael, *Mastering the Information Age,* Tarcher, 1991.

Ornstein, Robert, Ph.D., *The Psychology of Consciousness,* Penguin, 1975.

Penfield, Wilder, Ph.D., *The Mystery of the Mind: A Critical Study of Consciousness and the Human Brain,* Princeton University Press, 1975.

Rossi, Ernest, Ph.D., *The 20-Minute Break: The New Science of Ultradian Rhythms,* Tarcher, 1989.

Singer, Jerome, Ph.D., *The Inner World of Daydreaming,* Harper, 1975.

Smith, Adam, *Powers of the Mind,* Summit, 1982.

Smith, Robert, *Learning How to Learn,* Harper, 1981.

Stine, Jean, and Camden Benares, *It's All in Your Head; Amazing Facts About the Human Mind,* Prentice Hall, 1992.

Talbot, Michael, *The Holographic Universe,* Harper, 1991.

Witt, Scott, *How to Be Twice as Smart,* Prentice Hall, 1983.

The World Almanac and Book of Facts 1993, Pharos, 1993.

A

Active listening, 149
Affirmation, and OLS, 50-51
Allen, J. J., 144
Allen, Robert R., 163-64
Alpha-wave relaxation, and OLS,
    48-50
Alpha waves, 46
Ambiguous language, spotting, 132
Analogies, 133
Appeals to authority, 137-138
Apple Computers, mishandling of,
    175
Asimov, Isaac, 43-44
Assumptions, and inductive think-
    ing, 191-192
Attachment, 74-76
Audiotape, as learning resource, 64

B

Backtracking, 108, 113-114
Bad reading habits:
    backtracking, 113-114
    subvocalization, 110-111
    word-for-word reading, 111-113
Barbara, Dominick A., 146
Benson, Herbert, 49
Beta waves, 46
Body language, 170-172
    crossed arms, 172
    looking away, 171-172
    shift of position, 172
Boldface, and key ideas, 125
Books:
    as learning resources, 64
    reading, 107-108
Bottom-up learners, 58-59, 66

Brain:
    computer vs., 14-15
    secret powerhouse of, 19-21
    using other 90 percent of, 15-16
Brain starters, 179-80
Brochures, reading, 107-108

C

CD-ROM, as learning resource, 64
Change of subject, signposts
    signaling, 126-127
Charts, and key ideas, 125
Chesterton, G. K., 146
Coleridge, Samuel Taylor, 158
Committees, as learning resources,
    64
Compromise, 169
Concentration, 17-19
    and instant reading, 108-109
Conferences, as learning resources,
    64
Creative thinking, maxims of,
    201-204
Creativity:
    and IQ, 20
    and the unconscious mind, 20
Csikszentmihalyi, Mihaly, 32, 44,
    46, 146

D

Daydreaming, 203, 204
de Bono, Edward, 198
Deductive thinking, 187, 192-194
Deep breathing, and OLS, 47-48
Delta waves, 46
Dennis, Everette, 11

R

S

EDITOR: *Susan McDermott*

PRODUCTION EDITOR: *Eve Mossman*

INTERIOR DESIGNER/FORMATTER: *Dee Coroneos*

TYPEFACE: *11/13 Galliard*